ALSO BY SECONDE NIMENYA

Evolving Through Adversity

A Hand to Hold

A Leader's Companion Workbook to
Evolving Through Adversity

Address all inquiries to:

Seconde Nimenya
info@SecondeNimenya.com
www.SecondeNimenya.com

Editorial Review

**New Young Adult Book Tells African Girl's Story
of Survival and Her Triumph in the Struggle
to Get an Education**

A Long Way to School tells the remarkable life story of Seconde Nimenya, a woman who grew up in Burundi, Africa.

Nimenya is the author of three other books, including *Evolving Through Adversity,* her award-winning memoir. *A Long Way to School* is her young readers edition of that book, rewritten to inspire middle and high school age readers to overcome the challenges in their own lives.

Seconde Nimenya's story is one of relentless determination in the face of challenges and a constant desire to learn and rise above her circumstances, no matter the odds.

From her early life, Nimenya refused to give up. As an infant, she crawled into a fire when her mother left the room for just a minute. Her parents had to carry her to the nearest hospital, an hour away by car, but since they didn't have a car, they did the trip on foot.

Whether it was dealing with poverty and not being able to afford the mere necessities, fighting to get an education, walking everywhere she went, or dealing with the bullies in school and in life, Nimenya never gave up. Her resilience through much adversity is what made her who she is and informed her mission in life.

A Long Way to School is the story of fulfilling a purpose despite the difficulties. I doubt any reader in North America has experienced the hardships Nimenya did in getting to school, but she was determined to succeed, and she did. Eventually, she married and moved to Canada and then to the United States. She went to college, and perhaps most amazing of all, the girl who didn't even know what a book was as a child, grew up to be a writer. She is now the author of four books and plans to write many more.

A Long Way to School will open the eyes of anyone to the privileges we take for granted in public education in the United States. As Nimenya writes in the book, "I believe education is the only solution that truly empowers communities and has the potential to end the cycle of poverty and violence."

Her commitment to education, the obstacles she overcame, and what she had been able to accomplish will be eye-opening and inspiring to young readers. Nimenya's message is one of hope and encouragement. She believes that with determination, people can always achieve their dreams. No matter how difficult the journey, she tells us to "Always be persistent, like I was, even though it was *a long way to school* because I knew when I got there, it would be worth it."

A Long Way to School is a wonderful book for young readers everywhere. It would be a perfect reading assignment for history, social studies, and English classes. In addition to sharing her story, Nimenya shares some leadership insights, in the "Ten Leadership Habits for Your Teen Years and Beyond," for readers to develop. She also provides a set of "Reflection Questions" at the end of the book, so readers can apply the concepts and ideas they've learned to their own lives, helping them figure out their own purposes in life and the futures they want to create for themselves.

Seconde Nimenya's writing style is easy to read, and suitable for young readers from middle school grade level to older readers. The cover suits the book well because it shows a little girl struggling to walk to school, when school was so far away from home—a literal and figurative image of what Nimenya's life has been. Read what this young girl has endured, and you will understand how you can also make the best out of any situation through perseverance.

I highly recommend *A Long Way to School*.

— Tyler R. Tichelaar, PhD and award-winning author
of *When Teddy Came to Town*

For more information, visit: www.SecondeNimenya.com

A Leadership Book for Young Readers

A LONG WAY TO SCHOOL

A Story of Overcoming Challenges and Never Giving Up

SECONDE NIMENYA, MBA
Author of *A Hand to Hold*

Library of Congress Control Number: 2019905707
Paperback ISBN: 978-1-7331124-0-6
Kindle Edition ISBN: 978-1-7331124-1-3

Nimenya, Seconde, author.

A Long Way to School/Seconde Nimenya. - Young readers.

1. Nimenya, Seconde -young readers. 2. Leadership 3. Education 4. Biography - Juvenile literature 5. Women- Equality, girls' education, economic empowerment 6. Africa- school, social impact, young readers 7. Self-help.

Editor: Tyler Tichelaar, Superior Book Productions
Interior Layout & Design: Fusion Creative Works
Africa Map: VectorStock.com
Burundi Map: Kelisi
Author photo: Sandra H. Matthews

Our books may be purchased in bulk for educational purposes.

Address all inquiries to:
Seconde Nimenya
info@SecondeNimenya.com
www.SecondeNimenya.com

Printed in the United States of America
First Edition

For my family

With Love,
Seconde

Note From the Author

This is a work of nonfiction. All facts, conversations, people, historical events, and places mentioned in this book have been reconstructed to the best of the author's recollection. Distances are estimates in equivalent miles. This book is not a history or politics book. Any reference to historical or political contexts serves as reminiscence of the events that have impacted the author's life directly or indirectly, in that time and place. A few people in the book are identified by pseudonyms; everyone else is identified by their real names.

Contents

Prologue

OFTEN, WHEN I SPEAK to audiences of young people, particularly students, they ask me how I became an author. They ask, "Did you like books when you were growing up?" My answer is, "No." As a matter of fact, not only did I not grow up reading books, but I didn't even have books in my school, let alone my house. Also, we had no libraries. The first time I saw a library was at the university. Books to me were a foreign object considered to have been invented by white people. The first time I touched a book was in sixth grade. The book was written in French and its title was *Bourgot*. It was so thick and filled with math problems from algebra to geometry. It was a very intimidating book. Its title might as well have been *The Book of Terror*.

Bourgot was the only book the school gave us in sixth grade, in preparation for our sixth-grade national exam that qualified us to enroll into high school in seventh grade. That is how our school system was designed. Americans usually call middle school grades six to eight. For us, sixth grade was part of primary school (what Americans call elementary school), and then we began high school in seventh grade. And since we were taught in French, and I hadn't yet mastered it, since it wasn't my native language, *Bourgot* was a tough book to use. We had no dictionaries, and no *Google* either! So, you can imagine how hard the math problems in *Bourgot* were to me.

When I started seventh grade, the school owned a few books, mostly donated by foreign countries such as Belgium (the former colonizer of Burundi, my native country in Africa). That year in seventh grade, our teacher assigned us a book to read for which we had to do a book report. That was the very first time I was asked to read a book and do a report on it. This assignment was terrifying to me. So, here is what I did: I didn't read the book. And here is how I did the report: I copied word by word the book summary from the book's back cover, and gave that to my teacher as my book report. I know what you're thinking, "Did the teacher find out?" Do you really want to know? Yes, she did. Big time! And I got in trouble for copying the book cover and making it my own report. That is called plagiarizing. Yuck! Right? So, don't you try that at school. It won't work.

Not only did my teacher find out, but she made me redo the report, after I had actually read the book. Once I read the book and redid the report, I got a decent grade, but the teacher penalized me for turning my assignment in late, which was fair, to be honest.

This experience taught me a lesson: I made up my mind that from that day forward I would develop an interest in books, especially in stories that mirrored my own. I realized that reading was how I could learn from other people and visit other places I never dreamed I would see. By reading books, I could go anywhere the author took me. But because I didn't have access to many books, except the occasional ones given by our high school teachers, I eventually lost interest in books. That interest would only be reignited when I came to North America, where books are in abundance. That is when I found I couldn't stop reading.

So, when I tell my students that *no*, I didn't have access to books in my early childhood, they wonder what prompted me to become an author. To be honest, it is still a mystery to me. If you had told me I would grow up to be an author, I would have said, "Stop it; you had too much pizza last night." Because it is hard to dream of becoming something when you cannot see anyone else in your community or even your country doing it.

However, I believe we are all here for a reason, and because my purpose was to tell stories, even though I didn't know it, eventually I became a storyteller, writing books and speaking to share stories and encourage others. Today, I share with students that regardless of your life circumstances, you are here for a purpose that no one else can fulfill for you. You have a unique talent no one else has, and nobody can use your talent to do what you do, and the way you do it. You are unique. That has been the best lesson I learned after all these years of writing books and sharing stories. We are all put on this planet for only a limited time. We are given a gift, or sometimes more than one gift, but what we do with our gifts is entirely up to us. We have something called *free will*. Free will means you have the personal power to use your gifts. There is no obligation for you to act on your gifts—that's up to you.

Sometimes, it takes a nudge to use your gift. Other times, as has been my case, it takes a challenging situation, what is also called adversity, to make you act on your gift. Adversities come in different forms, and at different times in life. For me, the adversities I went through started in my early childhood. Growing up in a poor family with no money to afford the mere necessities for our family made me want to go to school and fight to get an education. Thus, when I was young, books were not a basic necessity, but a luxury that today many of us in the developed world take for granted.

When I finally had access to books, I realized the immense possibility of dreaming big dreams. But because of the different wars and the strife that had affected my native country of Burundi, people were afraid to dream. They lived in survival mode, and you cannot dream when you live in survival mode. The things many of us take for granted, such as books, are not even a possibility when you live in survival mode. You are worried about your safety, security, and how you can provide for your family. At the same time, those were the circumstances that helped me become more resilient. One of the things I wanted to share in this book is that people don't grow from comfort; they grow from discomfort, also known as growing pains.

When I first wrote my life story, titled *Evolving Through Adversity: How to Overcome Obstacles, Discover Your Passion, and Honor Your True Self,* I only focused on the adults who would read my story and hopefully be inspired by it. And it has been a rewarding experience to hear people tell me they could relate to my story, even though they had different life experiences. But, then, I also had young people, as young as middle school kids, who read my book because their parents shared it with them. Those kids told me they had learned a lot from my story of overcoming challenges, and never giving up. That is when I realized I wanted to write a young reader's version of my book to inspire you and other young readers on how to be resilient in your own lives, as you navigate your personal journeys.

My hope is that *A Long Way to School* will inspire you to rise above your own challenges, whatever they may be, step into your courage, do the best you can, and be the best you can be. You will learn how to run your own race, and not be concerned about what the popular kids do or think. As long as you are doing your best with what you have, that is already success, my friend!

On your journey, you might meet the bullies, both inner bullies and outer bullies. Your inner bullies come from your inner thoughts and your mindset. Do you know what the best part of facing those inner bullies is? The best part is you have control over what you feed your mind. Isn't that great news? I find it fascinating that you don't have to be concerned about what others are doing, as long as you are doing your best. And you know what is the other best part? I will tell you. The second best part is that when you feed your mind on good things, like good inspirational messages, your heart feels it and becomes peaceful. And out of your heart, you get and give good vibes, which is good energy that attracts good people and good circumstances to you. You see, you can feel at peace even when everyone else is freaking out, just by deciding to feed your mind on good mind-food.

Now, that is not to say that because you are a good person, you will not make mistakes or face some challenges. But being a good person will help you be more resilient and face those challenges head on. You will be more focused and find solutions to your problems more easily. And the third best part is that being a good person will also help you help others face their challenges. Isn't that the most awesome reason of all? At the end of this book, I will share a few habits you can develop to live peacefully with yourself and others.

Now, a word, or more like many words, on making mistakes. Mistakes, *yuck*. I know! No, no, not yuck. There is something nice in the mistakes we make. Mistakes are our best friends and not our enemies. Really! You know why? Because in every mistake you make, in every failure you face lies an opportunity for greatness. Failing or making mistakes makes you one of a kind. It means you didn't shy away from trying something new—from challenging yourself.

And the best part (yes, another best part, hooray!) of failing or making mistakes is that you can learn from your mistakes or your failures and do better next time. *Oh yeah, oh yeah, oh yeah, let's hula-hoop*. Here is an assignment for you. Next time you fail at something, just do some hula-hoops. Swing your hips a few times, and say, "I can do this!" Do this when you are doing difficult homework, or simply a task that seems intimidating. Just swing, and then start over and try to do again whatever you failed at, or fix wherever you made a mistake.

The reality is that you have to try new things and see how they turn out. Imagine if Thomas Edison had only tried once to invent the light bulb, and when it didn't work the first time, he gave up. If he had, I am not sure we would have electricity today. Maybe someone else would have invented it. I don't know. But you get the point, right?

Trying makes you almost perfect. Almost! The worst failure in life is not trying. If you never try, how do you know it will not work? So, what if it doesn't work? At least you tried. And oh, what if it actually works? You see, you would have missed by not trying. And that's what most people do. They try only one time, maybe just two times, and if they don't succeed right away, they give up. Well, not you; you are a never, ever *giver upper*. (Not a real word, I know, but you get the point).

The stories you are about to read in this book make up a part of my life journey. I share the life lessons I mostly learned from failing or making mistakes, or simply from coming from where I come from. These stories are also about how education truly changed my life. And most importantly, through my story, you will learn that through all the difficulties I faced from the time I was a baby, to my adult life, I never, *ever* gave up.

The fact that I grew up without books, but now I'm writing them is something more than I could have dreamed for myself. And if I succeeded at anything, it is because I took trying seriously. And I took seriously the thing called "free will." Remember that? Yes, I took my gift seriously, applied some free will, and BAM! I started writing books. I made many mistakes, and I failed many times. Oh, my gosh, of course I did! Wait, what? Was I supposed to be perfect? Oh, my bad. Well, guess what? I am far from perfect, and even if I were, my kids would never let me brag about it. Yeah, I have kids. I bet you didn't know. Here is the best part of not being perfect: *No one is.* Not you, not me, there is not one person on Earth who is perfect. Maybe on Mars, but not here on our planet.

If, while you read this book (and I hope you will, not just the cover like I did in seventh grade), my story makes sense to you in any way, take a highlighter and use it to highlight the parts that inspire you or cause you to say, "Huh, I didn't see it that way before!" Oprah says this all the time, why not you? To help you reflect on your own story and life, I have added some prompts in the form of Reflection Questions at the end of the book. You can answer the questions right inside this book. However, if this is a school book, please don't write in it or highlight. Instead, take a notebook, or better yet, a diary, and write down your thoughts and reflections in your dear diary. That way, you can share what you learned from the book with your friends and family.

Happy reading!

AFRICA

Africa is the world's second largest continent, and has a multitude of languages, cultures and subcultures, and a rich and beautiful landscape with amazing wildlife.

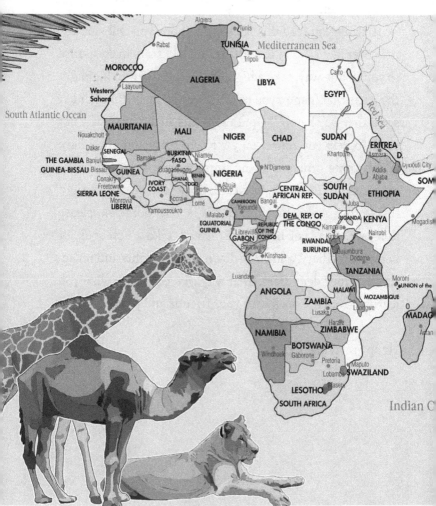

CHAPTER 1

Rising from the Ashes

ONCE UPON A TIME, I was a baby in a crawling stage. One day, I was home alone with my mother. It was lunchtime, and my mom was preparing food for our family, a meal we called *ubugali* in Kirundi, my native language. *Ubugali* is made from cassava, corn, or wheat flour, all staples locally grown in my native country of Burundi, and in many other parts of Africa. To make *ubugali*, you boil water, add the flour, and mix it using a long wooden spoon. You mix and mix until the flour and water become one good mixture, and no more water or flour can be seen—only a big thick ball of *ubugali*. I grew up eating *ubugali* because it was the most affordable food for many families. It is very high in carbohydrates and, therefore, a good source of energy. To eat *ubugali*, you take a slice (usually eaten with the hands) and dip it into meat stew or beans mixed with green leafy vegetables, which was far more affordable for many people. That is what my mother was making that day—*ubugali*.

My mom momentarily left the area, where there was a fire for cooking and a pot of boiling water, to get the flour in another room, leaving me—the crawling baby, in charge. But I did not want to be left in charge, so I crawled and followed her. I took the shortcut in her direction, tripping and falling into her pot, which was three-quarters full of boiling water. Oops! The water spilled into the fire, creating enough smoke to burst all smoke alarms (but we had none). Double oops! And I, the crawling baby, dipped my entire left side of my body: face, arm, and leg into the gleaming fire. I was having a staring contest with the embers. That fire burnt my small and fragile six-month old body.

I don't even know how long I was in those hot ashes. When my mom returned with her corn flour, she found me grilling to the bone. I can imagine the awful guilt she felt when she realized she should have known better than to leave a crawling baby beside a fire and boiling water.

I was immediately (I hope) rushed to the nearest hospital. Now, when I say nearest hospital, I'm stretching it a little. It wasn't near. It was located about an hour's drive away. And that was under normal traffic and road conditions, combined with having a car. But my parents had no car. They had to walk to that hospital. I learned from my older siblings that my burn was bad; I stayed in the hospital close to a year.

I wonder if I ever crawled again. I forgot to ask my mom. Probably not—who needs to be crawling, when all I did was crawl into a fire?

But time and the hospital nurses who were Belgian nuns (they were our best doctors) did a good job. I am happy to report that I fully recovered from the burn trauma and injury. I know I fought for my life with my left hand, because that is where I still have scars after all these years. I don't think those scars will ever disappear—a sign forever of how close I came to death.

Immediately following my release from the hospital, my mother took me to her parents. Although my stay there was supposed to be temporary, I ended up living with my maternal grandparents until I finished primary school.

When my grandparents took me in, I was a very small and fragile child. All the time of baby growth I was supposed to do during my primetime baby months was spent hooked up to God knows what in the hospital, preventing me from dying. Hey, I'm grateful for that!

My grandmother told me that one day, when one of her best friends saw me, she told her, "My dear friend, although you have been taking care of your daughters' kids, this one is going to be an exception." She implied that I would not make it. How rude!

Whenever I saw her, I wanted to say, "Hey, old lady, why were you saying mean things about me?" But I couldn't say that, of course. Although I'm sure my grandmother's feelings were hurt, my beloved *nyogokuru* (grandma in Kirundi) never held a grudge. They remained best friends as long as I can remember. Grandma made it her goal in life to return me to my parents in better shape than she had received me. My *nyogokuru* was pretty awesome.

Needless to say, my grandparents were poor. But it seemed to me that poverty wasn't even a word we used in my village. My grandmother and my aunts, who lived at home at the time, always managed to have something to fill our stomachs. I ate food we grew, and I drank fresh banana juice made from the bananas grown on my grandparents' farm. Unless Mother Nature was angry and provided too much or too little rain, we had enough food. At home, I sometimes wore my aunt Aurelia's oversized shirts, which became dresses for me. And on the first day of school, when I started first grade, I wore borrowed clothes from a neighbor's child.

In addition, we didn't have electricity. That was a luxury only afforded to a very few of the city people. Most of the countryside went to bed early (around 7 p.m.) because of the lack of electricity. The only occasional light we could afford at my grandparents was a lantern made from a can shaped into a small container called *ikoroboyi*, in which we poured kerosene. Kerosene is a gasoline-like liquid that smells awful. To make the light, we inserted a little piece of cloth, usually ripped from old clothing and folded into a knot that was easy to insert in the lantern and inside the kerosene. Then to light it, you just used either a match or a flame from the cooking fire and lit the tip of the small cloth. At my grandparents' house, it was always my job to go to the market to buy kerosene, and then come home to prepare the lantern before nightfall. To save on kerosene, we only used the lantern when we had guests from out of town, so we could feed and entertain them under the light. Also, adults used the extra-lit time to chat and catch up with our guests before bed.

Now it was understood that I couldn't use the lantern to study or do my homework. That wasn't a priority worth the extra expense on kerosene. And because we didn't have electricity, we relied on firewood not only for cooking, but also to heat our house, especially during the cold rainy months. This meant that every day after school, my other chore was to walk several miles to fetch cooking wood. All these chores left me with no time to study or do my homework after school. I didn't even bother taking my notes home because there was simply no time to study. I honestly don't know how I passed my exams with just what I had absorbed during class.

I realized that I came from a poor family that couldn't afford private tutors or extracurricular activities for me, or pay fat bribes to the school administrators like some of the rich parents did to let their kids advance without merit. I solely relied on my effort in class, and I did the best I could. And it was hard. The irony was that some of the kids who came from well-to-do families struggled in school, despite their parents' efforts to get them the privileges their money could buy.

But as long as I didn't go without eating for a day, we weren't really poor, or so I thought. In addition, my grandfather had cattle. He had close to a hundred cows from when my grandparents had first moved to the southern region. The southern regions had caused many cattle owners to migrate because they sought greener pastures, which were in abundance in the lower lands and valleys, where there weren't too many people yet. Even though there was rich grass in the lower lands of the south, cows didn't tolerate well the summer's heat and humidity. Also, there were too many bugs compared to the hilly sides of the country. Therefore, my grandfather's hundred cows died one by one. By the time I was ten or eleven years old, we only had ten cows left.

All my grandfather's attention was given to his cows. Each time a cow was sick, we didn't take it to the veterinarian, oh no! My grandmother was the cow doctor. She did her best to make the cow medicine out of herbs and other plant leaves. She tried different kinds to get the cure, but sometimes, she couldn't find the right combination, or she only found it when it was already too late for the cow.

Although life was not easy, we had everything, or, at least, I had everything I needed. I had grandparents who loved me unconditionally, cows that filled our compound, and baby cows that occupied half of our house. We had cats too, lots of them. I didn't like them because they slept in my bed, and sometimes, they had babies right there in the corner beside my bed. We didn't know that they triggered Grandma's asthma attacks. I only have this fancy knowledge now. When I look back, I remember that my grandmother never had a break from her asthma. And since we had cow milk, cats were there to indulge themselves, drinking my milk. As a little girl, I hated milk. Whenever Grandpa was milking, Grandma would try to force me to drink warm milk fresh out of the cow. The milk was still warm, with bubbles on top. But I couldn't; I just couldn't drink it. Here is how I tricked my grandmother so she would leave me alone. I would take the warm bubbly milk, go in hiding, and spill it on the dusty floor, or in the kitties' milk container. Occasionally, I drank skimmed milk. Do you know how to skim milk? I will tell you how we did it.

Skimming, to separate milk from cream, was an elaborate process. We used a churn, called *igisabo* in Kirundi. First, you pour milk into the churn, and in a circle motion, you agitate the churn for about an hour, or until the butter granules form. Then you drain the milk into a separate container and put the butter in another container. Aging the butter was also a long process that consisted of putting the butter in a covered container, placing it in a cool dry place, and leaving it untouched for months. When it was considered ripe enough, my grandmother would put a small slice of butter in the food as a condiment. It would melt in, and it was actually yummy! That was the only type of butter my grandmother consumed, because she had health issues that limited her food choices.

At my grandparents' house, my daily chores consisted of fetching cooking wood and carrying water from the pond (three miles away). When I turned ten, another chore, the one I hated the most, was added to my list: leading the cows to the pastures. Leading cows to the pastures on the hill or across the valley from our house was the worst! One day, one of our cows wanted to teach me some type of lesson about daydreaming. I must have been on cloud nine when I found myself on top of the cow's horns and up in the air. Usually, when a cow picks you up like that, it shakes you in circular motions and then throws you at a distance. I was afraid to call for help because I didn't want to make the cow more nervous. Fortunately, before the cow started shaking me on its long horns, a neighbor, who was herding his cows on the same pasture, saw the scene and rushed over to rescue me from the cow. Seeing my neighbor coming toward it, the cow bent its head and dropped me on the ground. I landed with only minor injuries.

That day, I hated cows! I wished them all to be slaughtered right away so we could eat their meat, and I would be freed from leading them to the pastures. But, of course, no matter what the cows did, my grandfather wasn't going to let that happen. And it's not what I wanted either. If nothing else, I liked our cows for filling our property; they gave me a sense of security, as if the cows were our security guards.

That special cow was a tough one. One time, cow thieves came to my grandparents' house in the night and stole all our cows, except that one. It had chased them away, and even woke my grandparents up by running around, making noises, pushing the fence, and knocking on the house's door with its horns. We named that cow *Bihayi*, which can be translated as "glory" in the Kirundi language. To find our cows, my grandparents called out to the neighbors to help and they all followed in the cows' footprints. Five miles away, the thieves heard the people following in their tracks and calling out, so they gave up and ran into hiding. My grandparents were able to bring our cows back home. It was the scariest night of my youth! Back then, stealing cows was the ultimate threat against cattle owners. Many cattle thieves did it as a profitable business, and they attempted stealing my grandfather's cows many, many times, but our *Bihayi* always chased them away. Sometimes, the thieves brought salt to tempt the cows to follow them, because cows crave salt. But the tough one always kicked them away, and they finally gave up.

After my incident with our proud cow *Bihayi*, my grandparents released me from cow-herding. That chore left to Barenga, my adopted aunt (she had been adopted by Grandma as a child). My grandmother preferred to send me to fetch water and firewood. Every day, Grandma said to me, "Sakunda, it's time for me to start cooking dinner. Go to the pond to fetch me water." My grandmother called me *Sakunda*, because she couldn't properly pronounce my name. Even though I didn't like it, I had given up on correcting her.

I would grab a bucket and walk to the pond. I liked fetching water because at the pond, I met other kids my age and we played games in the water. I would get myself wet from head to toe while trying to catch tadpoles. Some of the older girls said that if you got a tadpole to bite your nipples, your breasts would grow instantly. Some of my friends had started growing boobs, but I still had a flat chest. So, I needed all the help I could get. Despite my efforts, I never caught one tadpole; they were the fastest thing in water. One day, I had so much fun playing with the other kids at the pond that I forgot I was supposed to bring water to my grandmother. *"Oh, no! I'm in so much trouble!"* I shouted as I realized we had been playing for hours.

When I got home, my grandma was very angry at me because she needed water to start cooking dinner, especially when she was making dry beans that took hours to cook. "Sakunda, where were you all this time...? Where were you, child?" she would scold me each time I came back with a bucket half-full of water, because I had spilled it all the way home from the pond as I tried to rush. She would only yell at me, and she was never upset for more than a minute, letting my grandfather be the bad cop.

"Sorry, Nyogo. I won't do it again," I said to Grandma.

Whenever I misbehaved, my grandfather chased me with his walker and hit me with it on my behind. I drove him crazy by running from him and hiding.

"Child, come back here! Sooner or later, I will get you!" Grandpa would threaten because my hiding worked up his anger. And until he had given me a good correction, he never gave up. Unlike Grandma, he never let me get away with anything. Even when I hid from him for a day, he would still punish me whenever I reappeared. And whenever my grandfather started whipping my behind, my grandmother defended me.

"Leave that child alone! What will I tell her mother? She entrusted us with that child!" Grandma said between coughs and wheezing due to her chronic asthma.

"You tell her that you spoil this child rotten. That's what you will tell her mother, or I will!" Grandpa menacingly said.

Although my grandparents never knew it, I was terrified that they would tell my mother I was misbehaving when she visited us. I prayed that they would forget to tell her about my mischief. The idea of telling my mom on me sounded like a way to make me suffer more. I had heard my big sister Claire talk about my mother's disciplinarian methods. In those days, hitting a child wasn't considered child abuse; it was tough love. At times, only corporal punishment could reach me and make me behave. I know, I was such a handful of a child. But now as a parent myself, I realize that since my grandmother didn't discipline me that much, I needed the balance my grandpa provided.

Despite his harsh discipline, Grandpa loved me, and I still have sweet memories of him. His way of showing me love was to always give me leftovers from his food. Even when I was full, and he wasn't. It was how he showed me his affection, and I loved it.

Grandpa was also my favorite storyteller, especially at bedtime. He used to tell me stories of the big-headed monster (*igisizimwe*) that chased ill-behaved children. Those stories didn't actually help me fall asleep; they scared me and kept me up at night. So, the next day, I would try to be on my best behavior to avoid being eaten by the big-headed monster. And that is how we learned—by adults instilling values and other teachings into our young minds, through the power of storytelling. When I came to the United States and realized how many Disney movies were based on fables like the ones Grandpa used to tell me, I was like, "Wow, Grandpa, you were way ahead of your time." Especially after watching the movie *Beauty and the Beast*, memories of my grandfather's tales came back to me.

Grandpa also taught me to pay attention to worldwide events from an early age. He believed that happenings in other parts of the world affected us even in our remote village. He was a world news consumer, listening to the radio my uncle had bought for the family, but over which Grandpa quickly established sole custody. No one else was allowed to use the radio, or God forbid, talk during the news broadcast.

At news time, Grandpa would say to me, "Child, go bring me the radio." I would bring it and open it for him, making sure it was turned to the one and only channel we had. I would then sit down beside Grandpa and listen to the news with him. This was my favorite time spent with my grandfather. On the news, I would hear how some leaders around the world were treating their people. Some well, and some not so well.

I will never forget the first time I heard about a country called the United States of America, and a president named Jimmy Carter. The name *Jimmy* sounded really beautiful and fancy to my ears. I had never heard that name before. And so, when my uncle and his wife had their first baby boy, they said to me, "What name should we give to the baby?" They put me in charge of naming their baby. Guess what name I gave to my little cousin? I named him Jimmy! Obviously, after President Jimmy Carter.

Through listening to the world news on my grandfather's radio, I developed an awareness that I was a citizen of a much bigger world. I learned that *me* or *us* in my village also meant *them* or others out there in the world. I learned that humanity was interconnected, and it opened my views of the world beyond the four walls of my village. And I thank my grandfather for that gift. He gave the gift of mind expansion and a curiosity to want to learn more and dream.

When my grandparents got older and less mobile, disciplining me was left mostly to my aunt Aurelia before she got married. She wasn't much of a hitter, but one day, she gave me the lesson of my young life. I was in third grade, and my two best friends, Sera and Media, and I started playing games and getting to school first an hour late, then two hours late. We would leave home early in the mornings, meet up at our meeting place, and walk very slowly, talking and playing, so that we forgot we were going to school. After two or three days of this routine, we eventually started not showing up at school.

One day, we were so late that we saw students coming back home after school while we were still on our way. We then turned back and headed home as if we had been in school. Our parents never suspected what we were up to until, a week later, when the school principal summoned them to come meet her and all our teachers. When the letter requesting my grandparents to come to my school was sent home, I instantly knew I was in double trouble. Although Media and Sera were also in trouble, I was the only one who didn't live with my "real" parents, so I knew whatever punishment I was in for would be doubled once my mother heard about what I had done.

Aunt Aurelia answered the summons and took me to school that day. After she was briefed on my case, she went in the nearby bushes, cut a fresh switch off a tree, and hid it behind her back. She took me in front of the class, in front of my teacher and my classmates. Then she whipped my behind, while repeating, *"Uzosubire!"* "If you do that again...!" That is not a fair translation, because when said in Kirundi, it is a real threat. I started to cry. "Swallow your tears!" Auntie Aurelia said. It wasn't the physical pain that made me cry. It was the humiliation of being beaten in front of the whole class. From that day on, I promised I would be a good student and never mess around again.

Except...this one other time, when Aunt Aurelia taught me some good values through the power of myths. As a little girl, I learned a myth that cattle owners believed. They believed that if you drank cow milk or ate food mixed with cow-derived butter, then you could not eat some other foods, such as palm oil, because it would make your cows sick. One time, I ate food with palm oil at my friend's house, and later, I forgot and drank skimmed milk at home. When I realized what I had done, I was so frightened of what would happen to our cows. But I kept silent from fear Grandpa would punish me. What if the myth was real and Grandpa's cows got hurt because of what I had done? Grownups told scary stories to children that if we did such things, and ate the forbidden food, the cows' udders would fall off. Nothing of the sort happened, of course—at least nothing related to what we ate. So, quite often, I took on the habit of challenging this myth by eating what was forbidden, just to see what would happen. What an angel I was!

But my actions didn't go without consequences. I was once apprehended eating a fancy donut (called "*mandazi*" in Swahili) that I had been given by one of my friends at school. She was from the Swahili community where they made those donuts to sell. I saved it until I got home, and I was enjoying it when Aunt Aurelia saw me.

"Where did you get that thing?" she quizzed me.

"I got it from my friend Amina at school," I said, my voice shaking in anticipation of her punishment.

"You naughty child," she said, grabbing my arm. "Don't you know you'll cause the cows' udders to fall off? Do you want your grandfather to know about this? Why did you eat that kind of food?" Aunt Aurelia demanded.

"But..." I started.

"No buts! Give me that thing."

She took the rest of my sweet donut and threw it far into the fields. And then she gave me the spanking of my life. When she was done, I ran and hid for a while. Thank God she didn't tell Grandpa. Even Aunt Aurelia was afraid of my grandfather's punishment for me. From then on, I decided that if I was ever fortunate enough to get another sweet donut, I would never show it to anyone. I would finish it at school and come home clean. Those donuts were the sweetest thing I had ever tasted.

To this day, I still don't understand why there were such myths among cattle owners. What I do understand, however, is that drinking milk was a lot healthier for me as a little girl than eating the *mandazi* full of saturated fats and loaded with sugar. Many such myths were used to teach good habits and other values to children.

Although my grandmother was sweet and tried to shield me from many things, including the spankings my grandpa and my aunt gave me, she couldn't shield me from everything. Sometimes, she had to let the universe take care of me. And that is exactly what happened the day she told me to go unleash our calf, which was grazing in the fields, and bring it home.

I must have been ten or eleven years old when this happened. The sky had started turning gray, then dark, and seemed bloated and ready to explode. Everyone was in an alert mode. I was going to bring the calf home when, suddenly, I fell into a ditch and lost consciousness for a few seconds. Then I woke up and smelled a weird smell on me. It was difficult to identify what kind of smell it was. I thought it smelled like something burnt. But I could not quite identify it. It smelled maybe like, burnt plastic? Minutes later, I felt a burn on my left forearm and realized I had been struck by lightning. But I was too weak to make any move. I started calling for help, calling my grandma, "Nyogokuru, Nyogo... Grandma..." but my voice was too weak to be heard over the thunders. I waited in the ditch to regain composure and, eventually, some strength to call for help. Then I saw another bolt of lightning, followed by the sound of angry thunder, and my whole body felt like a lifeless mass.

Barenga, my adopted aunt, started calling me and looking for me everywhere. I could hear her call my name, and I answered, but my voice was too weak for her to hear me. I also heard my grandmother calling me, "Sakundaaaaa...!" I could hear how anxious her voice was, like she wasn't going to lose me to lightning strikes now, when she had already saved my little life as a toddler suffering from burn trauma.

I made the Sign of the Cross in a very grownup way. It was like I knocked on God's door and said, "Please, God, don't let me die and disappoint Grandma." At that very moment, I heard my aunt Barenga come toward me, running frantically. She picked me up from the ditch and brought me into the house. She put me on the floor, and by then, my grandmother was crying nonstop.

The lightning must have really zapped me because my whole body was so weak that it felt like I had no bones and no muscles to hold my little body together. My grandmother and Barenga, and whoever else was on the scene, started calling my name to revive me. Their calling went on and on for several minutes. I could hear them, but I felt both present and absent, as if I were floating in a world I didn't understand. But I wasn't in pain. After a couple of minutes of them calling my name and reviving me, I tried to be strong for Grandma. I wanted to speak, but words wouldn't come out. Then I tried to reassure her with non-verbal signs that I was alive, but just a little weak. I wanted to tell Grandma I wasn't dying. That I only needed to sleep, to get a little rest. But my grandma was too anguished to pay attention to what I was trying to communicate. I could tell she had already lost hope that I would survive the lightning strike.

So, I just stayed on that floor, waiting to regain strength, as I watched Grandma cry endlessly. I don't know what I did after a moment, but then, everybody stopped calling my name. They started to relax and were relieved I had made it.

I later told my grandmother that it was kind of nice to have a sneak peek to see who would cry if I died. (Naughty child, even at my deathbed, huh?)

Whew! There I was, revived and alive. My blood started flowing at its normal rate again. I started telling my grandmother and my aunt what had happened, and how God had saved me because I made the Sign of the Cross. My grandmother started putting some of her traditional medicine on the burn that the lightning had left on my forearm—the very same left arm that had been burnt when I was a crawling baby. It was the only part affected by that tropical storm.

After two weeks, the burn started developing an infection. I went to the clinic near my school, even though there was a traditional belief that it was bad to use modern medicine for burns caused by a lightning strike. I went to see a clinician despite my grandmother's pleas never to use modern medicine. I guess I had an attitude at that age, so I would not listen to her. The nurse put some cream on the burn, and it healed the very same week. The clinic staff congratulated me on beating the lightning and staying alive. I still have the scar on my left forearm. Each time I am upset by something, I take a look at the scars on my left hand caused by the burns from when I was six months old, and the scar on my forearm caused by the lightning strike. Then I remember how God saved me from dying at such a young age. Nothing can snatch you out of God's hands if it's not your time to go. You were created for a purpose, and God will make sure you fulfill it.

BURUNDI

Nicknamed, the "country of one thousand and one hills," Burundi is one the world's smallest countries. It has a beautiful and diverse landscape, mild temperatures, beaches on the shores of Lake Tanganyika, and is home to some of the world's most exotic birds.

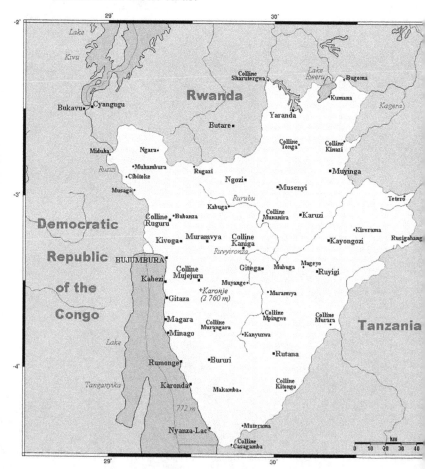

CHAPTER 2

Origins

MY NAME IS SECONDE NIMENYA. My last name *Nimenya* roughly translates as "only God knows." In my native country of Burundi, many last names include God, especially for Christians. Others however, reveal how a family is coping with life's circumstances. You may hear names with a victory meaning, or names with a victim meaning.

On the other hand, my first name, Seconde, takes its roots from the Latin name *Secunda*. My mother was a fluent reader of the Latin Bible, which was introduced in the early nineteenth century into Africa by the Roman Catholic Church. Although my family calls me Sekunda (they dropped the C and adopted the K for easy pronunciation), in high school, students started to call me Seconde, pronounced *"Segonde."* Seconde is the French version of Secunda, and I ended up keeping it. In French, Seconde means the second born, but I am the fifth out of seven children. Maybe my mom thought

I would be the second from the back, but then she decided to have two more children after me, and so, I'm the third from the back. Huh, interesting!

As if my name doesn't sound mysterious enough, I also have to contend with a mysterious English accent. And in my early days of coming to the United States, I struggled with sticking out as different. Sometimes, it was because people made insensitive jokes or asked stereotypical questions. For example, one guy asked my husband, "Do you guys have houses in Africa?"

So, I started adopting some coping tactics. Whenever people in the United States asked me, "Where are you from?" I would simply reply, "I'm Canadian." One day, my two teenage daughters sat me down, looked me in the eyes, and said, "Mom, we've noticed that each time people ask you where you come from, you lie." I knew it was getting bad when my teenagers decided to have an intervention for me.

While some of the questions came from people who were insensitive or ignorant of other races and cultures, I also met many nice people. People who asked me real questions about my origins because they genuinely wanted to connect with me. They wanted to learn something new about the places they had never been, or people they had never met. My kids were smart enough to realize my coping skills were slowly hindering my personal growth and ability to connect with others.

Do you know what I decided to do? I decided to turn all those bad experiences of feeling different into teachable moments. I realized I couldn't control what other people say or how they behave. But I had the power to choose how to respond.

Yes, you've got the power! You see, when something unpleasant happens to you, you have two choices. One: you can be bitter, or two: you can choose to find the good in the situation. Remember the *free will* I talked about in the beginning of this book? Yes, that is what I meant. You get to choose how to respond. You always have choices in how to respond to situations.

Instead of being bitter about people being mean to me and my family because we were different, I chose to speak up. Not shouting, but using my words to educate others about how it's okay to be different. Our differences, known as diversity, make life more interesting. I started writing and speaking on the topics of diversity and inclusion in schools, colleges, companies and communities. I realized that when people have a problem with you because you are different, it says more about them. It has nothing to do with you; it's their problem and not yours. I realized that when people have insecurities about who they are, they will try to unload on you to make you feel inferior so they can feel superior at your expense. That is what happens when someone is not happy with their own life; they look for people and situations to blame so they will not need to work on themselves and take responsibility for their lives. And that is what happens with most bullies.

Of course, we are all different, and that's a good thing! But we also have more in common than what divides us. Have you noticed that dividing people is so easy? But try uniting them; it takes work. My response became that of bringing people together, uniting communities and sharing different perspectives that make people relatable to one another. It doesn't matter what is your race, gender, sexual orientation, religion, or nationality. The way you are is exactly how God made you.

The realization that the way I am is exactly how God made me helped me to integrate into American society. I started to let my guard down and share with people where I came from—my origins.

"I come from Burundi," I now tell the people I encounter. If they are interested, I then share a little bit of Burundi's history and even politics. I don't think many people in North America know that Burundi is even a country. Sometimes, I, myself, have a hard time finding Burundi on the African map because it's a tiny country. Take a look at the African map at the beginning of the book. Burundi looks like a little dot, a drop in a big ocean, as one Burundian song used to so eloquently put it.

When she was in middle school, my middle child Elva told me that she learned about Africa in social studies. "That's a good thing, sweetie!" I said proudly. But then Elva added, "But it's too boring, Mom. We can't wait for this subject to be over!"

I bet it was boring. It bored me too when I was in high school learning about those weird names of old African tribes. What teenager in his or her right mind needs to learn about the *Mossi* Empire or the *Mandingue* tribe? We were also asked to memorize country capitals in a song, and that's how I still remember a couple of them. We had to memorize the names of presidents around the world, and the names of all of Burundi's government officials and other high-ranking politicians. At every change of government, they changed the officials, and we had to start all over again.

Only after I was grown did I realize what a wealth of knowledge I had about the world in general. So, I told Elva she should strive to learn about Africa because it is the second largest continent both in area and population. For people to understand my story, it is important that I first share about the country I was born and raised in.

Burundi is a small landlocked country located in East-Central Africa. Burundi was nicknamed "the Heart of Africa" because of its almost heart-like shape and its central location in the African continent. It is bordered by Rwanda on the north, the Democratic Republic of the Congo on the west, Tanzania on the east, and Lake Tanganyika to the southwest. Burundi covers only 10,745 square miles with a population of a little bit over ten million per a 2012 estimate. The weather in Burundi is temperate, which means it is not too cold or too hot. Only Bujumbura, the major city and capital located alongside Lake Tanganyika is hot and humid.

When it comes to the climate, Burundi is a paradise on Earth. Its evergreen forests, mild temperatures, lakes, exotic birds, and endless hills offer an enjoyable panorama that has long been the envy of many Westerners.

Kirundi and French are Burundi's official languages. Swahili is spoken mainly in Bujumbura and other commercial centers, and it is often a language of communication between Burundians and their eastern counterparts, such as Tanzanians and Kenyans.

Today, Burundi is economically one of the poorest countries in the world. Although there was a very limited number of wealthy people when I was growing up, my family was not among them. We were poor and we struggled a lot. I grew up in a mud hut, with dirt floors, no electricity, no running water, and no indoor bathroom or toilet. No video games, no television, no iPhone or iPad, no *i* anything for that matter. And no mall, people! School was a rare luxury usually only allowed for boys.

Like most rural families, my family farmed for a living their whole lives. And not with tractors and trucks like the farmers in rich countries like the United States and Canada, or in Europe. No. They farmed, and still do, using a tool called the hoe. It takes a lot of time and energy to break up the soil using the hoe. I hated using it when I was young because I always hurt my toes with it. From plowing to planting or seeding, until harvesting, my family and I were always busy with the farm work. Most people woke up at dawn to work in the fields, before the sun rose, because it would get too hot. In addition to working in the fields, my family raised cattle, and it was a lot of work doing farm work, helping with home chores, and going to primary school when I lived with my grandparents.

My hometown where my parents lived and where I was born is in southern Burundi, in the province of Makamba. My parents have always lived in Vugizo, a small town in the southwest of the province. Vugizo's nickname is "la Suisse" because of its similar landscape to Switzerland. It is a high rough plateau on the side of a group of mountains, Mount Inanzegwe being the highest in my hometown region at 7,000 feet elevation. The climate in Vugizo is also a little chillier than in the lower landscapes of the rest of the province of Makamba.

In Burundi, we have four seasons. The big rainy season is from December to April. The big dry season is from July to August. The months of September to November are called the small wet season because it rains, but not as heavily as in the rainy season months. Also, the months of May to June are called the small dry season because it is dry, but not as dry as the months of July and August.

My hometown's main challenge was the lack of good roads due to its geographic landscape. Because of the rough mountains and hillsides surrounding the town, it was always difficult to build decent roads. There was only one bumpy road that connected to Vugizo, no matter what direction you were coming from. So much for being like Switzerland!

But during my university years in the capital, I was always excited whenever I reached that bumpy road on my way home to visit my parents. The landscape of mountains and endless hills was breathtaking. It felt like home to me, and I wouldn't have traded it for any other place.

However, after living in North America for a while, I complained a lot about the road's conditions when I visited my family in Vugizo. After many years of enjoying the comfort of North American roads and highways, I felt discomfort on the bumpy road. Those traveling with me kept apologizing for the road's conditions, as if it were their fault. They also asked me to compare the road to the ones in the United States or Canada. Well, where should I have begun? Should I have described all the highways and interstates? How about the beautiful bridges? But I knew what their questions implied. How could this tiny country, their beloved Burundi, not have decent roads like we have in Canada or the United

States? I simply told them it was impossible to compare Burundi to North America because of the differences in their economic development. Fortunately, the bumpy road was only an hour's drive, and before I knew it, we were at my parents' house.

I once visited my family with my son Darrel, when he was a little boy. He was so amazed by what he saw that he still talks about it in awe. For him, seeing cows, chickens, and goats up close and personal was the most amazing experience he ever had. And I was happy that at six years old, he was able to experience the difference between his life in the United States and life in Burundi. He had a blast and appreciated everything he saw. Darrel surprised me with how he adapted to the people he was seeing for the first time. I especially loved seeing him bond with my mother, even though he didn't speak Kirundi, my mother's language, and my mom was unable to speak English or French. But the two communicated their love through a non-verbal language. And wherever my mother went, Darrel followed. To me, this was a testimony that love truly doesn't speak any language. Because love is the language.

My son took every opportunity to run outside and play without the restrictions I usually put on him when we were in the United States. He felt free to talk to strangers for no particular reason. Darrel thought anyone who was black was related to us. In my hometown, my son and I were special guests. All my neighbors came to welcome us, and they even danced for us till the wee hours.

I was amused by one of my neighbors, a man in his late seventies who knew a thing or two about riches. He said to me, "So, tell me, my child, I hear America is beautiful. Is it true that it's sparkling and has marble everywhere you go?"

"Oh yes, marble is everywhere!" I said. I couldn't bring myself to spoil his enthusiasm and knowledge about America. In another instance, Darrel was the one particularly impressed. On our way back to Bujumbura (the capital city) from my parents' house, we met school kids in their khaki uniforms going back home. It was a wet day. It had been raining steady for three consecutive days. This was February, the middle of the rainy season. Our pickup truck got stuck in the mud and couldn't move. Some of the kids were my son's age, if not younger. But they climbed on the pickup truck as it kept sliding in the mud and moving in spirals. One of the kids yelled at our driver, "You don't know how to drive? Pass me the wheel!"

Despite their apparent poverty, those kids seemed happy, loud, and free to be just kids. Most of them didn't get to see cars up-close often, which was why they came to our spiraling pickup to experience the spectacle when they saw it moving slowly. The driver had to chase them away to get them off the vehicle, and they ran giggling.

Those kids reminded me of my elementary school years. Those early times when I would walk two hours each way to go to school, with my big sister Claire yelling at me because I wasn't fast enough. Some days, I just couldn't take it anymore and would drop on the ground crying. Claire would grab my hand and literally drag me behind her. I would tell her, "I can't run anymore; my tummy hurts." It was true. But my sister didn't believe me. She thought I was lying to force her to walk at my slow pace. Well, sometimes I lied to get her to walk at my pace. Every time we were late at school, our teachers hit us on the legs and even the head with a stick that they kept in the classroom for that occasion; and each time, my sister blamed me, of course.

Back in those days, schools were only found at major commercial centers, where Arab merchants had established communities before Germany and then Belgium colonized Burundi in the early twentieth century. The colonizers had then built schools following the established commercial centers. When I was in elementary school, it was very common in many parts of the country to only have one primary school within twenty to thirty miles, and we had no school buses. I walked to school since I was in the first grade, every day, six days a week, on bare feet—rain or shine.

CHAPTER 3

An Innocent Mind

IT ALL STARTED WHEN my maternal uncle, Uncle Apollinaire, decided to enroll me in primary school and pay the school fees. Unlike in Western countries, to attend primary school in many African countries, you had to pay school fees. And I also had to buy a uniform. I attended a girls-only primary school called *École Primaire des Filles de Makamba* (Makamba Primary School for Girls). The primary school for boys was located not far from our school, and we had the same uniform color. For girls, it was a blue skirt and a white shirt, and for boys, it was blue shorts and a white shirt.

Aunt Aurelia had been preparing me for first grade admission by teaching me math skills. She showed me how to count from one to twenty, using my fingers and toes. One day, she sat me down, demonstrated for me, and then said,

"Now it's your turn. Add up all your fingers."

So, I started counting. "One, two, three, four, five, six, seven, eight, nine, ten!" I said proudly.

"Now, add your fingers to your toes, and in the same way, count how many you have together," Aunt Aurelia told me.

I did as she asked, and magically, I could count to twenty, using my fingers and my toes. It was the first time I realized I had ten fingers and ten toes. Quite a discovery!

The day before school began, Aunt Aurelia said to me, "I will take you to school on your first day." But there was one problem: I didn't have nice clothes to wear for my first day of first grade. So my grandma said, "I'll ask Nelda if you can borrow some of her daughter's clothes for your first day." When my grandmother asked our neighbor Nelda, she said, "Yes, of course!"

The next day, Nelda brought me a skirt and a shirt that belonged to her daughter Sera, who was also starting first grade at the same school as me. When we started school, Sera and I became fast best friends, until I graduated sixth grade. Sera failed sixth grade and got married the following year.

On the first day of school, I noticed there were many students. And I noticed something else: Some of the students wore nicer clothes and even wore shoes. I did not wear shoes—I never wore shoes my whole childhood. That was the first time I realized how poor my family was. It made me sad to see that my family didn't have even a little money to buy me a new dress for my first day of school, much less shoes like some of the other kids at my school. The first time I wore shoes, I was in seventh grade, and they were flip-flops. Before that, I walked barefoot everywhere I went.

I decided there and then that I would study hard in school and be somebody one day. Then I would have enough money to buy myself nice clothes and nice shoes. I also thought to myself, *"One day, I will build a nice house for my grandparents, and get them out of this thatched hut that has a leaking roof whenever it rains."*

But because I was a girl, I didn't know how I could achieve that dream. Back in those days, girls were not expected to attend school or dream fancy dreams like buying nice dresses and shoes. Finding a husband and having numerous kids was the ultimate achievement expected of girls. Did you know that even today, there are still many countries where girls are not allowed to go to school? There are also many countries where girls as young as ten or eleven years old are forced to get married, and sometimes to men old enough to be their fathers. So, I was one of the lucky girls who could start regular school because my maternal uncle agreed to pay my school fees.

Before I became school material tough, I had lived in a little cocoon world, protected by my grandmother. All that changed in April 1972 on a day when my big sister Claire and I should have stayed home. Instead, we woke up early as usual, packed our lunches, and walked the usual two hours to primary school. Claire was in the sixth grade and I was in the first.

Around mid-morning that day, parents began dropping by the school one by one, entering the principal's office. Then, I saw a parent come to our classroom, and my teacher went to talk to the parent outside the classroom, after she carefully closed the door behind her. Then the teacher came back into the classroom, called out one student's name, and told her to join her parent who was waiting outside. The student in question stood up, gathered all her school belongings, and left.

Next thing I knew, another parent knocked on our classroom door, and our teacher answered. She stepped outside the classroom, carefully closed the door behind her, and went to talk to the parent. On and on, the same scenario occurred.

Young as I was, I jumped to one conclusion: *Oooh, the little girl is in trrrouble! Na-na, na boo-boo, stick your head in doo-doo!* Okay, I didn't say that, but I thought of it. However, the way my little classmates gathered their belongings made me feel a little uneasy. We always left our notebooks and chalkboards in our desks at school, so when I saw my classmates leaving one by one with all their belongings, I thought they must have been bad students. Little did I know that this day wasn't an early dismissal day, but a bad day for my people and my beloved country. Those parents who came earlier to pick up their kids had heard that there was an ongoing attack in Burundi.

Shortly after, the principal called all the teachers and informed them that the rest of the students had to be released immediately. That is when we learned that some militiamen, *Mayi Muleles* as they called themselves, had started killing people in some areas of the country, including my parents' hometown. Men and boys were the main targets. My father was away in a different country in East Africa, so it was left to my mother to protect her children.

Grownups said that this war was an *ethnic war* between the main ethnic groups, *Hutus* and *Tutsis*. You see, in Burundi, there are three ethnic groups: Hutus, Tutsis, and Twas. Tutsis and Twas are the minorities, while Hutus make up the majority of Burundians. But they are the same people, living the same life, speaking the same language. To understand where all this hatred between the ethnicities came from, I will have to share a little bit of history with you. And that is in the next chapter, Chapter Four.

Although the word went out that Hutus were attacking Tutsis, it didn't register in my mind. I didn't feel any fear. As a first grader, I didn't know what ethnic group I belonged to. It was something my grandparents never talked about. Only later did I learn we were Tutsi, and that the mother with a mental illness and her daughter Barenga, whom my grandparents had adopted, were of Hutu ethnicity. I suspect my grandparents didn't talk about ethnic matters because they were an all-inclusive family. I never heard them mention the words *Hutu* or *Tutsi*. My grandparents respected every human being for who that person was, not what they might be. These were the early values I was brought up with. Many of my childhood friends and most of my classmates were of the Hutu ethnic group. Therefore, I connected with kids my age regardless of their ethnicity.

How could a kid my age understand that people were killing each other in the name of ethnic belonging? Sometimes when I think back to that day, I realize something about those parents who came early to pick up their kids. They were rich parents who lived near the city center, not far from our school. They were informed of what was going on in the country because they were members of our province's administrative branch. The other group was of Hutu ethnicity, so they knew about the civil war because they had been involved in its preparation.

But the majority of Tutsi students, like me, and even some Hutu students who lived far away from the school didn't get picked up. And our parents never got the memo about what was going on in the country. We didn't know what was going on until the school decided to release the rest of us all at once. Then we were told a war was going on between the government army and the militia mobs, the so called *mayi mulele*. We had to go straight home immediately.

My sister Claire came to my classroom and grabbed my hand as if I had caused the trouble. She instructed me that we had to go home right away. We were among the many kids who didn't get picked up earlier, and since we were released all at the same time, we seemed to fill the roads, running in every direction to get home. On our way, we met some military trucks transporting military forces wearing military uniforms, and camouflaged with leaves and grass on their military hats. It was a scary scene for any young child, but I wasn't scared.

Because of my childhood innocence, I didn't think about what the bad guys would do to us if they got hold of us. Who would want to kill a little girl? In addition, I relied on my big sister to protect me. Claire always defended me against the bullies at school. However, my sister seemed troubled because she understood what was going on. Older kids explained what was going to happen from bits of information they had. In my brain, it all sounded like waves from an unfriendly river. I couldn't focus or make sense out of it.

I heard someone mention that the militias were recognized by their chanting *"mayi mulele,"* so I started a song in my head with the words *"mayi mulele."* That little song got me in big trouble when I started singing it, first in whispers, and then out loud. Claire heard me singing and yelled at me, hoping I would stop. But the song was so stuck in my head I couldn't stop myself from singing it.

I didn't know those were bad words or even dangerous words because they identified the bad guys. But Claire took on the assignment of making sure I stopped singing those ugly words. She started hitting me each time I sang, and that is what it took to get me to stop.

When we arrived home, it was early afternoon. My grandparents had already learned about the war from one of our Hutu neighbors. My grandmother was afraid of what might happen to us. She looked at my sister and me with frightened eyes, not knowing how she would protect us from the killings.

The Hutu neighbor who had informed my grandparents about what he knew reassured my grandfather he would never hurt us. We were practically the only Tutsi family in our village. So if the Hutus in our village wanted, they could have killed us overnight and no questions asked. Instead, they continued to be the good neighbors they had always been. They viewed my grandfather as someone they could count on when they were in a difficulty, especially with regards to land conflicts. Grandpa was their *umushingantahe* (wise man)—a mentor they called upon to help them settle their problems. My grandmother also helped their families whenever they fell short on food. She would go to the family farm, harvest as much as she had, and split it into shares. She would then appoint me to bring some food to many of our Hutu neighbors.

If we ran out of salt before the next market day, I was sent to our Hutu neighbor to borrow salt for the night. For Burundians at that time, borrowing salt was a strong sign of trust. Because salt was a rare commodity, people didn't waste it by giving it to you if they didn't trust you would do the same when they had a shortage of it. In addition, the lack of salt showed some vulnerability that only your trusted friends could know about. We had a very good relationship with our Hutu neighbors, and we were grateful they didn't turn against us, as happened in other parts of the country.

Many Tutsi families had already been killed elsewhere in the country. It was just a matter of time before the war would reach us. Many Tutsis fled their villages in anticipation of what was going to happen. As soon as the radio started broadcasting news, my grandfather glued his ear to the radio. We learned from the news that some Hutus had taken machetes and killed their Tutsi neighbors. It was reported that this war was an act of ethnic cleansing to create balance in the government and the army. But those who perished were poor villagers who barely knew anything about politics or army matters. Again, all this sunk in my head, once I was old enough to understand during the subsequent wars. But at that time, I didn't feel any danger. I relied on the adults to protect me.

That night, we didn't sleep in the house. Everybody was hiding, and so did we. Hiding places consisted of nearby bushes, where we slept under the moon. Grandpa was concerned about his cows, but we left them home where, surprisingly, they stayed still, as if they, too, sensed the danger. Aunt Katarina, one of my mom's sisters who lived across the valley from us, joined us with her five children. I was very excited to see my cousins, but kids were quickly told not to move a finger. We were told to be on our best behaviors or else.

However, my grandmother's asthma attacked her with a vengeance. She coughed all night long. That was the only time I was scared that the bad guys might locate us and kill my grandma. Other than that, I felt as if we were summer camping, only it was April. April in Burundi is a month of heavy rain. Usually rain in April is accompanied by thunderstorms, heavy winds, and flooding. Indeed, we had rain that night—a lightning thunderstorm, so we were forced to retreat to the house.

We later learned that the Hutus had purposely started the war in April because of the heavy rain. They wanted to force Tutsis to stay in their homes. My parents' hometown was severely affected by the war, and we were very worried that my mom and my siblings might have been killed. We continued to try to live normally during the day. Adults continued to attend to their normal labors. Then we resumed hiding at night, as if death only came in the night. The nights were very dark, especially in the countryside, where we didn't have electricity.

By the end of July 1972, my grandparents' hometown, Makamba, was clear of danger. It wasn't as affected by the war as other regions in the south because most of the population there was of Hutu ethnicity.

On the other hand, reports said that in the south of Burundi, one of the most affected towns was Vugizo, my parents' hometown. My mother ventured out, took my five siblings, and came to Makamba to take refuge at her parents' house. We were so happy to see them alive. They had escaped by hiding in the mountains during the nights, especially Mount Inanzegwe, where many lives had been saved. During the day, they went home to continue their regular chores, and at night, they retreated to the bushes and mountains. They told us how my three brothers would have been killed if my mom had not disguised them in girls' clothes.

She told us about one particular close call. One day, my mom and my siblings had come home for the regular day's work and to make some food to take to their hiding place. Mom had dressed my youngest baby brother in a cute little dress she had borrowed from one of my little cousins. She had just put him on her back when a member of the militia groups (who was also one of my parents' neighbors) appeared out of nowhere and summoned my mother to show the baby's sex.

"That baby must be a boy," he said. "Let him off your back and let me check."

"No, she's a girl, don't you know?" Mom replied.

"I am sure that baby is a boy. Now let him off your back, or I'll kill you both," the militiaman threatened my mother.

"You better kill me first before you touch my baby," my mother challenged the man.

They argued back and forth for a while, and miraculously, the militiaman gave in and continued his man-hunting elsewhere. By then, both my older brothers, Cyriaque and Emmanuel, had slipped into a long hole they used to ripen bananas and covered themselves with banana leaves. They could barely breathe in the hole. The killer approached the hole and walked right by it, but he didn't see them. That's how they escaped.

This manhunt was believed to be the Hutus' strategy to eliminate Tutsis from procreating. They thought that by killing all Tutsi men and boys (including babies) and marrying Tutsi women, they would enable Hutu-only offspring and the population would be all Hutu in subsequent generations. Many Tutsi women were already assigned to Hutu men who would marry them after their husbands had been killed. My mother was assigned to some Hutu neighbor to take her once the war would end. My paternal aunt Domitila's husband was also hunted down and nearly killed by his Hutu neighbors who were competing to marry my aunt. They said she was the most beautiful woman in the village, and they almost killed each other while arguing over who would marry her.

Some of my relatives died, as did many of my classmates' loved ones. My Hutu best friend Sera's two brothers were killed while away at boarding high school. Many Tutsis and Hutus alike were killed in the name of ethnic belonging, and similar wars continued to haunt Burundi for many years. For the longest time, I had recurring nightmares about the militiamen chasing me. I would wake up in a rush of terror and be happy to realize it was just a bad dream.

• CHAPTER 4 •

A Little History

THE BEST WAY TO UNDERSTAND the present is by looking at the past. As I promised you in Chapter Three, this chapter gives you a little historical context for my native country to help you understand the different events that have impacted my life since I was a little girl.

You have probably learned or heard about slavery in the United States and its origins. And you may know that the slaves who came to the United States were taken from the continent of Africa. But Burundi escaped slavery because it was not conveniently located on the ocean, like many of the West African countries. Most of the slaves taken to the United States came from countries located on the Atlantic Ocean.

Even after the slavery ended, the people of Africa were not free. They went through the colonization by European countries. Burundi, along with some other countries like

Cameroon, Namibia, Rwanda, Tanzania, and Togo were colonized by Germany in the late 1800s.

Before the Germans came to colonize, Burundi was already organized with an administration. It was a kingdom with kings, chiefs, and sub-chiefs. The kingdom was divided into territories and chief-towns, led by chiefs and sub-chiefs. Although in Burundian history, the royal families were identified as the upper class, set apart from the masses, they were considered to belong to the Tutsi ethnic group.

As I wrote in Chapter Three, *Tutsis*, *Hutus*, and *Twas* (also known as *Batwa*) constituted the ethnic groups that lived in Burundi for centuries. According to historians, those ethnic groups have inhabited Burundi for at least five hundred years. Batwas were the minority (1 percent of the population) and were semi-nomadic; they chose to live apart rather than mingle with the rest of the population. They claimed to have inhabited the Great Lakes region of Central Africa, as the first population living by hunting wild animals. Batwas never had any significant political role in Burundi, and they were often ignored in the political power balance. When I was a child living with my grandparents, Batwas used to come to our house to sell us pottery. They were very good pottery artists. They walked around semi-naked and lived in locations where outside influence didn't easily reach them.

Therefore, the two main ethnic groups in Burundi were Tutsis and Hutus. The people paid tribute to the king, called

Mwami in the Kirundi language. The king owned all the land, and the royal throne passed from father to son within the royal descent. This means you could aspire to becoming a king only if you were the king's son. It also means you could be a member of the royal family if you had royal blood in your ancestry.

They also had wars at that time. But the main wars were against the neighboring territories to extend Burundi's geographical boundaries. In the late 1790s, under King Ntare Rugamba, Burundi's size almost doubled.

In Europe, in 1914, Germany declared what would become World War I. But in 1918, Germany was defeated by what is called the *Allies*. The allies were made of many European countries that fought against Germany and won World War I.

In 1919, after Germany was defeated in World War I, the *Versailles Treaty* redistributed all German colonies. After Germany's defeat, Belgium, one of the Allies that had won the war, was given both Burundi and Rwanda to govern.

So, Burundi went from being colonized by Germany, to being colonized by Belgium. The divisions based on race and tribalism weren't on the minds of Burundians before the colonization. Back then, the Tutsis and Hutus didn't hate each other because they belonged to different ethnicities. It was something all Burundians accepted, and they lived together in harmony. Each ethnic group had chosen different occupations to earn their livelihood. Each group accepted its living conditions and produced what it needed on the tenured land. The land belonged to the kingdom, and Burundians were tenants of the land on which they farmed and grew livestock. Tutsis were usually cattle owners, while Hutus were farmers. This division of labor formed a perfectly balanced traditional economy in Burundi. The exchanges were a part of the economic system that allowed for obtaining what one didn't grow or make.

Unfortunately, it was that division of work that brought on a negative connotation during colonial times. Race and class surfaced because the European powers were used to having a class system. And in order to govern Burundi, colonizers introduced the same social division in classes. They got one ethnic group to look down on the other. This move was called "divide and conquer," and it was the colonizers' best strategy to divide Burundians so they could maintain their power.

This strategy worked very well for the colonizers because it purposely weakened the relationship between Tutsis and Hutus. In fact, it was used by colonizers in most of Africa, and resulted in people hating each other. Obviously, the well-established Burundian aristocracy was seen by Belgians as a superior class since it had governed Burundi for centuries. The division in economic activities became the Belgians' first criteria for class division. Hutus who had labored on the land for centuries were now seen by Europeans as the "masses" or lower class. Tutsis who tended to their cattle were said to have migrated from northern East Africa and were being treated as if they didn't belong in Burundi. This idea was based on some similarities between some Eastern-African tribes' way of life and physical appearances being similar to those of the Tutsis.

I suppose the migration literature might be true. Just like anyone else, Tutsis had to come from somewhere. But I never understood why the migration theories always stirred so much hatred among people.

Although Belgians introduced the school system as I came to know it in Burundi, they didn't leave much else as a remarkable legacy. The little development they brought to the country consisted of road construction and was done by the Burundian people. Colonizers also forced Burundians to cultivate crops for European consumption, especially coffee and tea. They also forced them to be their carriers and laborers and to pay heavy taxes. If Burundians broke the Belgians' rules, they were not just punished. They were severely beaten and publicly shamed. My grandfather used to tell me that in his time during the colonization, men were beaten up and forced to drop their pants and be whipped (with a big whip called *Ikimoko*) on their behinds until they bled.

Grandpa used to sing to me the song Burundians sang when, finally, the Belgians left: "*Ababirigi baragiye sangwa Burundi we,*" which means, "Belgians have left, glory to

Burundi!" It was a cheering song that celebrated the end of the colonization in 1962, when Burundi got its independence. However, the psychological impact resulting from the colonizers' dividing the two ethnic groups stayed within Burundians' collective conscious and, inevitably, caused Hutus and Tutsis to start fighting as soon as the Belgians left.

CHAPTER 5

The Shift

WHEN MY SISTER CLAIRE left school after she failed sixth grade, she went to live with my parents for good. I was the only one left living with my maternal grandparents, whose health was deteriorating daily.

For the first time at school, I had to look out for myself since my big sister was no longer there to protect me against the bullies. Although I had occasional visits from my cousins who lived nearby, I mostly felt like an only child. I started longing to live with my family and all my siblings. I missed my sister Claire, and even her bossing me around.

As soon as my sister left school, bullies were everywhere! My best friends, Media and Sera, and I were constantly harassed by older boys from the neighborhood. One group of boys followed us every day after school. We did our best to run from them, but they ran faster, and sometimes they threw rocks at us. We were afraid to tell our parents about being bullied because the bullies were boys. Our parents would have assumed we were flirting with them, and we would have been the ones in trouble.

In my culture, girls were always the ones in trouble because we were told to avoid boys, and especially, not to "provoke" them. As a girl, whenever you reported being harassed by a man or a boy, your parents said something like, "What were you doing with him? It's your own fault; why were you with him in the first place?" Our parents rarely took a girl's side or questioned the boy or the man's motives. So my friends and I knew better than to tell our parents about our boy trouble. We were sure they would never take our side.

We thought about reporting those boys to their school administrators. But then, we found out they were school dropouts. We knew where they lived, but we were too afraid to tell on them to their parents. This bullying went on for several months, until one day I told my friends, "Hey, we need to stand up for ourselves and stop the bullies from harassing us."

"Are you crazy? How are we going to do that?" they replied.

My friends thought I was out of my mind even to think we could stop the bullies, especially since I was the tiniest of us three. But I insisted we had to do something if we wanted to stay in school and alive. At that point, I knew I needed to stay in school and achieve some level of education. I didn't want Uncle Apollinaire's money to be wasted. I had been committed to pursuing my education ever since I had gotten in trouble for skipping school in third grade.

One day, my friends and I were leaving the school and going home. We were anxious as usual about meeting the bullies. Some days, they hid around the block in the back of the school, making us think they weren't coming that day, so we would start celebrating. But then, we would see them resurface out of nowhere to frighten us. They didn't hurt us so much as just make us feel anxious and exhausted from running away from them.

That day, after I had told my friends we would stand up to the bullies and they had agreed, the bullies came and started following us. As soon as we saw them, Media and Sera started running. So much for standing up for ourselves! But I refused to run. I stood there and faced the bullies. When one of the boys started touching my hand, I pushed him. Then I said, "I am going to report you to my parents, who will tell my school, and the school will tell your parents. You guys are going to get in big trouble!"

How I thought about that I don't really know. All I know is that I felt like David facing Goliath. After a couple of minutes of this confrontation, they gave up and ran, calling me names. But that didn't bother me that much. My friends had been watching the whole confrontation from a distance. They looked like frightened chickens and were amazed that I had managed not to get killed. They couldn't believe that tiny me had saved them from the bullies. That day, we ran home, happy and free. The bullies disappeared altogether, and we never saw them again.

Now that I was older, I could make the trip to school in about an hour and half, mostly running. I had to leave early every morning. I remember what my grandmother used to say to me: "If it weren't for your Uncle Apollinaire, you'd be attending catechism school and be nearly done." Grandma insisted that my entire school trauma was her son's fault. I can still see her saddened face as she woke me up every morning, wheezing from her chronic asthma and talking between coughs, calling me Sakunda. Catechism education was only two days a week instead of every day like the regular school. All I needed to do was take my first communion and my confirmation, and then no more studying, only attending Sunday Masses with Aunt Aurelia. In Catechism school, they learned how to write in cursive and read the Bible. My grandmother found regular school too hard, and she loved me too much to put me through that torture.

Grandma wasn't Catholic, but she believed in something bigger than herself. She mostly worshipped God through the elements of Nature and the greater universe. But she knew that for my generation, the time had come to be religious and belong to the new beliefs brought by Europeans. To my grandmother, even though I didn't need school, she knew I needed to receive the sacraments. After all, I had been baptized when I was only eleven days old.

Although Grandma didn't go to church or practice religion in the formal way Catholics did, she worshipped a Higher Power that she called God (*Imana* in Kirundi). I remember she always ordered that we keep clean drinking water in the house overnight because God might be thirsty when he visited us. Now that I look back at how my grandmother practiced her spirituality, I realize she used the same practices that today are considered forward-thinking for spiritual living.

But as a child raised in the full bloom of a Catholic school, I silently criticized Grandma's ancient practices. To me, they were not civilized because in the religion class at school, we learned that they were not. We were told that we had to get rid of those "uncivilized" practices our grandparents adhered to. To my generation, those practices were "way back."

Moreover, Grandma used supplications and affirmations in her world, asking the universe to be clement and provide the abundance her family needed. I witnessed this especially during the drought, when Grandma would say her supplications to ask for rain. Another time, Mother Nature was angry and sent us hailstones. Grandma burned some type of animal skin (I didn't even know what it was, but it smelled awful). She put the burning animal skin in front of our house to make the hail go away. She expected some type of magic just to take the hail away.

In my grandmother's time, these practices were used to sustain life and understand the universe's mysteries. I witnessed my grandmother bring witch doctors to our house to perform some sort of magic to deliver her from her asthma. But I always felt sad to see that, time and again, my grandmother wasn't cured by the witch doctor. Because they were poor and couldn't afford proper medical care, my grandparents and many of the village people resorted to witchcraft. And they were taken advantage of by people who claimed to have magical healing powers.

But I can say that my grandmother had some type of knowledge when it came to traditional medicine. She used to perform colon cleansings for herself and her grandkids whom she raised, using herbs and other medicinal plants. She would try to heal all my wounds and other booboos. Sometimes it worked; other times it didn't.

Uncle Apollinaire must have known more about education and modern civilization than his beloved mother. He had joined the army right after sixth grade, which was all it required to enlist. He earned the rank of corporal, which wasn't high, but he was known as a *muzungu* in our village. Muzungu means "white person" in Kirundi. You see, people in the villages didn't think there was any distinction between being well off and being white. Because in the army he was earning a little money, people saw my uncle as having the same advantages as a white man. His military career afforded him a better life than most in the village.

My uncle could send his parents some money for rice at Christmas. Christmas was the only time we could afford to eat rice because of the money my uncle sent us. You might think rice was a luxurious staple. It was for many people because we didn't grow rice in most parts of the country; most of the rice was imported from other countries. And that is why only those who had extra cash could afford to buy it. My uncle also used a nice-smelling soap called *Lux* that was imported from East-Africa (Kenya or Tanzania). I liked that soap a lot!

In addition, my uncle's military career allowed him to marry a southern belle, whose beauty was breathtaking. I know what you're thinking. *A southern belle, really?* Yeah, really! She came from the south, okay? Her name was Melanie. Melanie was eighteen years old when she married my uncle, and he was way older than her. Something like late thirties maybe. And as I grew older, Melanie and I became good friends. I was the one she confided in more than my aunts. She always treated me well and brought me treats after she had been to the market. She used to tell me she wished I could marry her cousin John, who was a high school senior at that time. Although I entertained the fantasy in my preteen mind, her cousin was way older than me, but then, to Melanie, that wasn't a problem.

I was protective of my uncle's wife. Because we were close, we went on errands together, and each time a man made a pass at her (and God knows men did), I would give him a disgusted look, and Melanie always thanked me. My grandmother was always a good mother-in-law to her. She treated her as one of her own children. And because Uncle Apollinaire was her only son, I had a feeling Grandma sometimes unintentionally favored Melanie over her own daughters.

My uncle put me in school because he had a vision of what it meant to be an educated person. He paid for my primary education up to sixth grade. That's all I needed to get through and beat the system. Had I been in the care of my own parents, I would have ended up like my oldest sister Eugenie. She was withdrawn from school by my parents to help them on the farm. Eugenie had been first in her class from first to fifth grade, but she had been pulled out of school by my parents to help my mother with domestic work and raise her siblings. My sister loved school, but she was not given the chance to continue.

Uncle Apollinaire only had the financial means to put me through primary school, which consisted of grades one through six. In sixth grade, we had to pass a national exam that assessed our admission into high school. In our class, I was one of the four students who passed the test out of approximately fifty students who took it. Even though passing this exam was a big deal in a kid's life, and I should have been excited, I was worried. Who was going to pay the high school tuition? It couldn't be Uncle Apollinaire. He had just retired from his military career, so he had no money to pay for my high school.

The locations where the students who had passed the national exam would be enrolled in boarding school were announced a month before the school year would begin. I had two months of summer vacation I was supposed to enjoy since I had passed the national exam. But I kept asking myself: *Am I really going to high school? Who is going to pay for it, and which school will I go to?*

That year, my beloved grandmother, the one who raised me, died and everything changed. Aunt Aurelia had married, and Barenga, my adopted aunt had also met her beau. I had shifted to being a caregiver to my grandparents long before Grandma died. Her health had deteriorated so much that I became the one Grandma and Grandpa relied on. Officially, my uncle's wife Melanie and I were in charge. But my grandmother never wanted to burden her daughter-in-law, so she turned to me for her care. She had battled her asthma for so long, and one day, she just stopped breathing. I only have selective memories of the day she died, probably because that is how I coped with her death.

All I remember is that Barenga had spent the night at our house. The next day around noon, she came home from the fields to eat lunch. Although Barenga was married and had a home of her own, she always came to help my grandmother with farm work. When she went to check on Grandma, I heard her scream. She had found my grandmother cold and breathless on her bed. I never went in my grandmother's room to look at her body. It was a good thing for me because to this day, I only have memories of my grandmother alive and not dead.

My cousin and I were sent off to tell our two maternal aunts, Scholastica and Aurelia, who lived seven hours' walking distance away. Since we had no telephones, it was the only way we could communicate their mother's death. When we got to Aunt Aurelia's house, before we could tell her the reason for our unannounced visit, I burst out crying. Aunt Aurelia immediately knew what had happened. She understood how I felt because Grandma had practically been the only mother I knew well.

Although I visited my paternal grandparents during the holidays when I was in primary school, I wasn't as close to them as I was to my maternal grandparents. My dad's father suffered from an illness I didn't understand at the time. His name was Daoudi (I think it was the equivalent of David). Whenever I visited Grandpa Daoudi, he never recognized me. My paternal grandmother, Regina, would tell him,

"Sekunda has come to visit us." But my grandfather only stared at her. Then she would repeat, "Sekunda, our grand-daughter, she is here to greet you." But he never seemed to understand.

Grandpa Daoudi was a strongly built man. Looking at his physical appearance, no one would have suspected that he wasn't well. He was tall, with strong leg muscles, and was very attractive for a Grandpa! I kind of felt hurt because I was used to the attention of my maternal grandparents. And this granddaddy wasn't excited to see me; he didn't even know who I was! I gave up on getting his attention. I figured my other grandfather would never ignore me. But, of course, Grandpa Daoudi wasn't ignoring me. He was the same with his other grandkids who lived on the same com-pound with him and played around him every day. He still didn't know any of them, and he always seemed withdrawn and far away. No one in my family understood what was wrong with him. But everyone seemed to accept it as an in-curable condition. Now I realize he probably suffered from Alzheimer's disease.

Despite her health issues, my maternal grandmother lived a long life, full of grace and love for those around her. Through her actions, she taught me empathy. She taught me to accept others for who they are. And she taught me that everyone deserved dignity and respect no matter their lot in life, or where they came from. I missed her love, which would follow me into my adult years, when I would look for love in all the wrong places.

Following my grandmother's death, things became different for me. I could feel a real shift in the air, but I wasn't prepared for the change. I was once again prematurely severed from my loved ones, and it seemed no one understood what I was going through. I kept the pain to myself from fear I would appear too needy for love and affection.

CHAPTER 6

Back Home

NOW THAT I HAD PASSED the national exam qualifying me to enroll into high school, and Uncle Apollinaire
realized he couldn't pay my high school tuition, he made a
decision. He said to me, "Seconde, your grandparents raised
you since you were a baby. And I put you through primary
school. But now, I don't have the financial means to pay for
your high school fees. So, it's time for you to go live with
your parents. They will decide whether or not they want you
to attend high school."

From now on, I was to be handed back to my real parents.
They would decide whether I would go on to high school, or
if I would stay home and work on the farm like my two older
sisters who had been pulled out of school. That certainly
wasn't what I wanted. I returned to live with my parents
with a lot of anxiety.

I can still remember the day I told my dad I had passed the national exam in sixth grade that qualified me to enroll into high school. Dad looked at me and said, "High school? What for? To be the next president?" So, unless I was studying to become the next president of Burundi, my father considered school a waste of precious farming time. Although I had passed the national exam qualifying me for high school, my dad wasn't anxious about how I would pay the tuition because he didn't intend to send me to high school. He never understood why my brothers and I were in school. School was something he had never needed to do as the oldest son in his own family.

"I didn't go to school. What do you need school for?" my father would ask me. To my dad, having finished primary school was already way too much schooling I didn't need as a girl. He would tell us kids we were in school just to escape the home chores (which at least in my case was true).

But I could see that my mother was determined for me to attend high school. She started talking to our many relatives and even total strangers, asking for help for me to go to high school. I prayed so hard that summer, saying, *Please, God, send me a miracle. Please make a way for me to attend high school!*

It was only two weeks before high school was due to begin when I finally received my miracle. My youngest paternal uncle, who was a military officer and understood the importance of education, even for girls, agreed to pay for my high school tuition for seven years (grades seven to thirteen). And that's how I was able to start high school.

I suspect my dad may have regretted not going to school. In my teenage mind, I thought he had tried to escape the farm work himself when he had gone to East Africa to seek work in Tanzania and Uganda in the early 1970s. I wanted to tell him that, but I knew better, so I kept quiet.

Up until that time, I had never "met" my dad in person. When I had visited my family while I was still living with my grandparents, Dad was still in Tanzania. I had left home before I was old enough to form memories of him. Although people said we looked alike, I didn't even know whether I would recognize him if we met. At some point, my father was believed dead because we stopped getting news of him, especially during the civil war of 1972. After the war, one of my father's younger brothers had gone to Tanzania to look for him, but he didn't find him. I wished I was grown and able to go look for my dad in East Africa because I longed to see him. Sometimes with my friends, I made up stories about my father because I felt ashamed of not having a dad like many of my friends in school.

Before I met my father in person, I idolized him a lot. I imagined him as a fun-loving and caring man. Someone who would bring me so many nice things, like dresses and shoes, when he would come back home from Kampala in Uganda and Dares Salaam in Tanzania. That's where he was supposed to live, at least the last time someone gave us his news. We were not even sure in which city in East Africa he lived.

Years later, all my idolizing of my father was proven wrong. I was disappointed in many ways. He came back home with no dresses and no shoes for me or my sisters, nothing for my three brothers either, and definitely, nothing for my mom. In brief, he came back with nothing to show for his long absence. How could he come back without any gifts for me or my siblings? And what would I tell my friends when they asked what dad brought me? I was devastated, but I told no one about my feelings. Nonetheless, I was happy to finally meet my dad. He was no longer some image in my mind; he was there in person. And that made me happy. And yes, I confirmed that he was my father! We looked very much alike; no need to take a DNA test.

When my dad was still away, my mom had stepped up and become mom and dad, raising the kids alone. She had enrolled my two older brothers, Cyriaque and Emmanuel, in school. She tended to the crops on the family farm and sold grains in summer to raise money to pay my brothers' primary school fees.

At one point, mom had to sell a cow to raise enough money to send my brothers to school and provide for the whole family. When my dad returned from East Africa, my mom never questioned his efforts or what he had been doing the whole time. Then she told him how she had handled the family during his time away, and that she had had to sell a cow so she could send the boys to school.

Dad wasn't pleased with this announcement. In my culture at that time, women didn't have the right to sell livestock. Only men did. And my mom had sold a cow in my father's absence? That seemed like a gangster move on her part! It was like mom was rebelling against the culture, a culture that in many ways disempowered women and girls. But she had no other choice since she was raising her kids alone. Dad started resenting my mom and us kids for asking him to pay our school tuition. There were a lot of fights in my home at that time, and I wished my mother could stand up for herself. But she just crashed under the abuse. Sometimes, my older siblings had to get involved in the fight to defend our mom. I was always scared and retreated into a corner away from the rest. I would block my ears, hoping not to hear the fights going on in my home. I never said a word, and my father sometimes praised me as the sweet child for not challenging him about his behavior like my older siblings did. I suppose I was trying to get into his good graces so he wouldn't hit me.

I just wished school would resume so I could go away before I got hurt. I loved school even more now, because it provided me with an escape plan. It was the only way I could stay away from my home's turmoil. There was no other alternative for me, but to succeed in school.

Dad's temper always deteriorated around the time school began. He didn't want to hear another word about school supplies or tuition money. Therefore, when it was time for me to go to high school, I didn't know who would pay for it. I was terrified to ask him for anything. My mother kept pressuring him to find a solution for me to attend high school, which only aggravated him. Some nights, I would hear him say, "Why can't Sekunda stay home and farm like the other girls in this village? What's so special about her that she needs to go to high school? To become a government minister or what?" (He had already lowered the standard from president.)

Here I was, finally living with my real family for good. But I didn't really fit in. Before, I had only visited my family during major holidays, and I had always felt like a special guest. Whenever I visited my family, it was like being in another state for a sightseeing occasion, so I didn't have to adapt to the culture. And it felt like another culture. My family even teased me about my accent because there are slight differences in how people from the lower landscapes talk compared to those from the highlands. So, when I went to live permanently with my parents, my siblings always irritated me by commenting on each word I said. They would correct me and make me repeat the "right and proper way" to say a word.

The other thing my siblings and sometimes my parents complained about was that I was a very spoiled child. And that had to do with my crying. Whenever they teased me, I cried. And then they teased me more. And I cried even more! Also, they complained about my labor hours. I wasn't necessarily good at farming with the hoe, and if I could, I would have avoided it altogether. But I had to do my share. Since they could see that I didn't like it, they complained some more, and I cried some more.

One morning, my father told me to hold a little calf so he could milk its mother. He knew I didn't like holding calves. They moved a lot, and once I had been hurt by a calf at my grandparents' house. The little cow's leg had bruised my ankle, and the bruise had turned into an infection that took months to heal. In my mind, I had made the decision to avoid holding baby cows while their mother was being milked. Calves are hyper; they just want to rush to drink their mother's milk. However, that day, my father put me to the task of holding the calf, and I made a terrible mistake and said, "No." Attitude!

My father made me hold the calf anyway, and then he said, "I'll see how many cows you bring me when you get married." He was referring to the custom of a man paying his future wife's family a dowry in cows. You see, in my culture, before a man could marry a girl, he first had to pay a dowry to her parents. At that time, the dowry was paid in cows, and the more beautiful a girl was, the higher the number of cows expected, and they had to pick the fatter ones. It went to show how much value the husband's family placed on their son's future wife.

I was infuriated when my dad implied that my only value in his eyes would be evaluated by how many cows he would get for my dowry, but I didn't tell him that. It gave me more resolve to fight even more for my education.

After a few months of being back home, I realized that while in my parents' care, I longed to be with my sweet grandmother. I found the strife in my family exhausting. I was used to living with my elderly grandparents who no longer had anything to fight about. My siblings seemed to notice I wasn't enjoying living with them, and they never tired of teasing me about it, which only made me feel lonelier. It seemed as if my siblings were all immune to the strife in our home, and no one could really understand my feelings. They certainly didn't miss my dead Grandma as much as I did. I didn't know what to do to fully fit into my family.

Also, everyone in my family seemed to be braver than me. For instance, at night, each of my brothers and sisters could go by him- or herself to the toilet (outside of the house), but I couldn't. Because of the 1972 killings in our hometown, I was frightened to go outside at night by myself. Usually, I would ask my oldest sister, Eugenie, to accompany me, and she did. But if I had been a bad girl that day, or disrespectful to her, my punishment came at night. She refused to go with me when I needed to go to the outhouse. And I knew better than to ask my bossy sister Claire. I couldn't ask my two older brothers because they were boys, and I was a girl; boundaries had to be enforced. I couldn't ask my two younger siblings either because they were still too young.

One night, I really had to go, and I wanted to show these people what I was made of. Gathering my courage, I ventured out by myself to go to the toilet. As soon as I set foot outside, my heart jumped into my throat. And as I looked at my surroundings, the banana trees became tall, mean men, wearing long and ugly brown coats, and huge and ugly old hats. They seemed to hold spears in their hands, but I couldn't see well. My family heard me wrestling with the door, trying to get back inside, but I felt a backward pull by the bad guys who certainly had followed me to the house.

By the time I made it inside, everyone, including my mother who was otherwise very reserved, exploded with laughter. Out of breath and with wild eyes, I tried to explain what I had just seen.

"I...I...I just saw men outside. There, they are there!" I said, pointing outside with no precise location. This only caused my siblings to laugh uproariously, until their bellies hurt. Then I felt humiliated because I had lacked the courage to go outside at night by myself—even this once. That's all I needed. A one-time courageous moment to beat the demons of fear.

Out of pity, my sister Eugenie took me back outside to do my business. She asked me to show her what I had seen.

"So, where are the bad guys you saw?" But, of course, the banana trees had regained their original shape, and no bad guys wearing ugly long coats and hats were in sight. We just laughed about the silliness of it all.

"There are no bad guys here. Not since the war of 1972. It's only in your imagination," Eugenie told me.

But her wise words were lost on me. I remained scared to go outside alone at night. Little did I know that out of all seven children, I would be the only one who would end up flying far...far away from home.

Although I longed for my dad's love and affection, I came to realize that he didn't know how to communicate his love and affection to me the way I needed. I realized that it was also the kind of upbringing he had had. In time, I was able to forgive my dad for what he had done or failed to do in my life. I know my parents did the best they could with what they had and knew. I am happy I was able to make peace with them and help them financially before they both passed away, when they were in their eighties.

Our parents may disappoint us sometimes because they are imperfect human beings, just as we are. I came to understand that every life experience gives you happiness and sorrows. You just have to be okay with all of it, learn from it, and be grateful for it.

CHAPTER 7

The Road to High School

I HAD BEEN LOOKING FORWARD to knowing what boarding school the Ministry of Education would enroll me in. By mid-August, the results of who passed the sixth grade national exam and their scores were announced. Along with the scores, students who passed the national exam were told what high school they would attend. The results were posted on bulletin boards at every major primary school district. When I went to look for my name, I found I had been enrolled in the Lycée of Gisanze, a girls-only boarding high school.

I had never heard of that school before. It was in the province of Muyinga, at the border of northern Burundi and southern Rwanda. Given my humble beginnings, traveling from my hometown to the school was going to be a huge pain in the neck, if I even went to high school. Even for those who had money, traveling from the south of Burundi all the way to the northern end of the country was a challenge, mostly due to the lack of transportation and good roads.

After I told my parents what school I had been assigned to, my father wasn't concerned. He knew I wasn't going anywhere. Who was going to pay for it? As far as he was concerned, I had already exceeded all expectations in education. I had achieved a sixth-grade education, and as a girl, that was more than I needed.

On my dad's side, we had a university graduate—my youngest paternal uncle, Vincent. He was my hero, even though I had not seen him yet. That's because he only came home occasionally for vacations, and each time he came, I was still in primary school and living with my grandparents in a different city. His vacations never coincided with mine. But I always heard that we had a very smart uncle. I felt I had to go as far in school as my uncle had. However, because I wasn't a boy, I knew there would be limitations. That dream of mine was far more achievable for my two older brothers, Cyriaque and Emmanuel, both in the ninth grade at the time. They were boys and likely to further their education. So far, they were proving all expectations right. Uncle Vincent had been paying for their high school fees.

Each time I gathered the courage to ask my dad, "Dad, am I going to high school?" he looked unconcerned. I could tell he didn't have a plan. Moreover, he was too proud to ask his younger brother, Uncle Vincent, whether he could pay for my tuition too, since he was already paying for my two brothers. My other paternal uncles all had many kids as well. It seemed as if we all counted on Uncle Vincent's kindness to pay our tuition, at least for those of us who went beyond sixth grade.

Not knowing what to do with me, since I wasn't good at farming with the hoe, my father finally asked my uncle if he could pay for my tuition, so I could go to high school. Uncle Vincent accepted, God bless his heart.

The high school where I was assigned was far away from my hometown: The distance between my hometown and where my school was located is approximately 500 km or 310 miles. Under normal circumstances, it would take me two days of traveling. But by Western standards, the same distance could be easily traveled only in a few hours on the highway system. But Burundi didn't have highways or even decent roads. No one in my family knew where the school was located, and no one volunteered to take me there. Again, under normal circumstances, my dad would have been the one to accompany me to boarding school. But if he did, it would have taken two bus tickets, or should I say two truck tickets? The country didn't have many buses; nor could my family afford the bus fare. My parents were struggling to send me on a one-way trip to my boarding school. They didn't have a plan for how I would return home for vacations. We would worry about that later.

The transportation consisted of commercial trucks, or sometimes pickup trucks would travel to Bujumbura, the capital of Burundi and its major city. From there, I would have to be loaded on another truck that linked Bujumbura to the province of Ngozi's city center before reaching my destination in the province of Muyinga. My school was in a remote village where missionaries had come since colonial times. There was one primary school, one high school (the one I was attending), a Catholic church, and one small outdoor marketplace. It was a very tiny village.

The part I looked forward to on that trip was seeing the capital Bujumbura for the first time. That's what I liked about this long-distance boarding school event. After that, I had no idea where I would go or how. Going to Bujumbura was going to be relatively easy since Uncle Vincent worked in the capital. That part of the trip was not going to be a problem. He had agreed to pay for my transportation ticket there. The road trip from Bujumbura to the school was still an issue, and my mother kept pressing my father to figure it out. Like another miracle sent by God, my mom suddenly thought of Ananias, the pastor. What an "Aha!" moment Mother had. Our neighbor, Ananias, was a Protestant pastor working as an evangelist in the province of Muyinga, where my school was located. He was trying to instill some Christianity into the people of a remote village. His preaching location was a few hours away from where my school was. He had just come for his summer vacation to visit his wife and kids who lived across the valley from our house.

Ananias was a man much known for his kindness, Christian religious teachings, and good heart. So, my mom went to Ananias' house to tell him about my situation and ask for guidance. She got blessings instead. Not only did Ananias know where the school was located, but he offered to take me there in person. "Hallelujah! Praise the Lord!" Mama said.

Here I was, starting a new chapter of my life, going hundreds of miles away from home to a remote school where modern civilization was still being introduced to people. It would be reported to me later that the region was better known for werewolves, witchcraft, and other black magic activities I have forced myself to forget over time. But because Ananias was going to take me to school, I stopped worrying for a while. And as if I had a lucky charm, his vacation ended the same time as mine, so we hit the road a week before school would begin.

The plan was to go to Ananias' preaching village first and stay there for a couple of days, waiting for school to start. In the meantime, I would be acquainting myself with the area. Then he would take me to school on his bicycle. Let me tell you something. It is one thing to ride a bicycle in your neighborhood, but when it's your only means of transportation to boarding high school, at least twenty miles away, it is no fun! I didn't even know how to ride a bicycle. Ananias was going to be in charge of riding the bicycle, balancing my life on his backseat.

The day Ananias and I met to start our journey for my high school adventure, we got a free car ride to Bujumbura. Ananias was well known in the community, and the few rich people in my village who had cars knew him. They all happened to be Protestants and businessmen, and he was their pastor. They would have driven him anywhere if he had asked. But he wasn't a man who took advantage of others.

When we arrived in Bujumbura at night, the city glowed! It was my imagined paradise. Lights at night make any city look glorious and glamorous. I was to be housed at the home of my dad's second cousin (maybe once removed). No, there is no such thing as "removed" cousins in Burundi. Family in Burundi is way larger than the mere limits of the relatives of your own generation. This structure is very constructive in many ways. Families help each other because if you look back in your family tree, the person you help might be related to you in the nth generation and is still called family. There is no such thing as "removed" relatives.

I spent the night at my dad's cousin's house in awe. There were so many firsts for me. It was the first time I entered a fancy house, with bedrooms and doors on each room. Each room, people! It was the first time I saw a toilet seat in white ceramic—and inside the house. Inside the house, people!

Ananias went to spend the night somewhere else with his Protestant friends, where they probably spent the night praying. (I was sure he would be praying for me without even being asked.) He was such a committed evangelist.

The next day, Ananias and I had to hit the road again. In the morning, he picked me up and we took the bus to the city's central market where the action was. It seemed to be the center of the universe. The central market in many African capital cities is where major economic activities happen. The transportation, shopping, foreign currency transactions, noise, pick-pockets—everybody was busy doing something or going somewhere. All the merchants had outdoor stalls, and their radios were blasting music to attract the customers' attention. And the chaos? Oh, my goodness, I loved it! This is what you miss when you grow up in a village.

Pastor Ananias and I took a bus called *"Hiace."* It was the size of a ten-person minivan, but not exactly as fancy. But in Burundi, it transported more than twenty people on a non-busy day. Thank God, we didn't have to take one of those big merchandise transportation trucks, in which you couldn't see where you were going that we called *"Tugezehe?"* literally meaning *"Where are we?"* Those trucks belonged to rich businessmen. They were packed with merchandise to the roof, and then people were loaded on top of the merchandise.

The main roads connecting Bujumbura to the province city centers were paved, and not too dusty. However, once we got off the main national roads (the equivalent of highways I suppose), roads were bumpy and dusty to boot.

So, it was glamorous only up to the province of Ngozi's city center. The province of Ngozi was located midway to Muyinga province from Bujumbura, the capital city. Once in Ngozi, we took link transportation—this time a pickup. But the driver and two other people who paid first class fare rode inside the pickup. The rest of us who purchased economy coach rode in the back of the pickup. And because the pickup had steel bars that allowed passengers to hold on, we were packed to maximize the return on investment of the Toyota pickup. Pastor Ananias rode inside the truck because he could afford it. When he looked at me from his front seat through the glass window, I could see pain in his eyes. He was probably wondering how my parents dared to send me to such a faraway land and not send anyone with me. I saw the look on his face, but I made it a point not to cry. Even though I felt a need to release emotions, I wasn't going to be a crybaby on my journey to being a high school student. *I had to grow up or else.*

I focused on the good I would reap one day. First, how I would grow taller, so when I returned home for the Christmas holidays, everybody would be amazed and say, "Wow! Look how much she grew in just three months!" Then

I fantasized about how when I returned home, I would go to church on Sundays, and all eyes would turn to me because that is what happened to high school or university students. After Sunday Mass, the crowd would just surround you and stare at you as if you were an alien, only cuter. I knew it would happen to me when I would go to church during the holidays. I could already feel the stares and some gossiping whispers. Because I didn't grow up in my hometown, many people didn't know who I was, except some relatives. Therefore, people at church would ask who I was and try to figure it out through my sisters with whom I went to church. This reaction always made me feel like an outcast right in my own hometown. The stares were annoying sometimes. People would check you out and talk on and on in whispers. But on that journey going to the pastor's house in Muyinga, I focused on the good, if only to avoid crying.

After we reached our destination, we walked about two miles to the pastor's house. As soon as we arrived, Ananias made sure he ordered his maid to feed me as if to compensate for the days I hadn't eaten healthy food in the past and the days I would not be eating healthy food in the future. But I couldn't eat anything. I just couldn't swallow food. The fancy bread, tea with milk and sugar for breakfast in the morning, and the good lunches and dinners prepared for pastors were all wasted on me. All the good food I used to wish we could eat at home was there, but I couldn't get myself to eat it. My heart was so heavy, and I felt a need to cry, but I didn't dare in Ananias' presence. He kept pressing me to eat, but I couldn't.

Ananias kept reminding me how important my education was for me and my family.

"You see my child, there aren't many educated girls in our village. It's important that you eat to be healthy and strong, and go to school and study hard," Ananias told me.

"But why me? Why do I have to be the hero for educated girls in my hometown? Why do I have to be the one going so far away?" I wanted to ask Ananias, but I could hear my trembling and broken voice before I even opened my mouth. So, I kept quiet.

Suddenly, I longed for what my grandmother used to say. "Had you just gone to catechism school, you'd be long done, child of my child." Plus, my dad said I had already exceeded expectations. I had finished primary school, and in his book, that was way too much schooling for a girl. So, why did I need the nonsense and trauma of high school? But here I was, and seemingly, Ananias wasn't going to let me escape. He had brought me this far, and his Christian religious beliefs encouraged him to seek a better life. He understood the importance of getting an education, while my own father didn't.

Sometimes, I had wondered whether being Catholic wasn't a setback for my family. All our Protestant neighbors seemed to understand the importance of seeking a better life for their families. They were always successful in business. The Protestant men I knew didn't drink alcohol, whereas some of the Catholic men drank too much. Compared to Catholic families, Protestant families also seemed to live in well-built homes—at least those I knew at that particular time and place.

The day Ananias and I were to leave for my final arrival to the boarding school, he readied his bicycle. He tied my luggage and sat me in the back of his seat. Then he told me, "Sweetheart, you have to hold really tight on my back, so you won't fall." Okay, so there was this possibility that I might fall into the street, while going to high school? Well, I held as tightly as I could. I held on for dear life, while traveling the bumpy streets of that remote village. He rode until his forehead started dropping beads of sweat. He rode until his back, which I was holding, became soaked with sweat. But he continued to ride for hours and hours on his bike without taking a break.

And finally, as we rode closer, I saw it. I saw my high school. We had arrived at my boarding school the afternoon before everybody else was due to arrive. Ananias had wisely decided that I would arrive at school a day early to get accustomed to the nuns who ran the school.

We introduced ourselves to the nuns. Ananias explained to Sister Marie, the headmistress, why I had arrived at the school early.

"I brought this child early so she can start getting used to the school's environment," Ananias told Sister Marie.

"Are you her father?" Sister Marie asked.

"No, I'm a friend of her family back home. I preach here in the province of Muyinga and was home for vacation when her family asked me to accompany her." Ananias couldn't possibly know how disappointed I was not to have my father accompany me. Instead, he became my father's substitute, even though it was my first time meeting this man in my hometown. I felt ashamed that we were so poor that my family couldn't afford to send anyone who was related to me to come with me on this important milestone in my young life. But I kept those feelings of shame and pain suppressed. I was doing everything I could not to cry in front of the nun.

Pastor Ananias eventually gave his contact information to the nun, as my guardian angel, should there be anything to report about me. I hoped there would be no problem, unless my school tuition wasn't paid. Where would I be sent then to be shipped back home? To Ananias's house, of course. Fortunately, Uncle Vincent had given me the tuition money for that first trimester. I just needed to put my little brain to work and get through that first term.

Sister Marie was a beautiful and tall nun. She wore a long dress that hung slightly below her knees, a pullover, a nun's veil, and open sandals—all white. She looked very much together and in command, and I instantly felt I could both trust her and fear her authority. I learned later that she was very strict as well. She introduced me to the head matron, Sister Helen, another tall nun who was the head of dormitory affairs, food matters, and everything related to the school's logistics. And that was no small job, considering that the lycée housed close to five hundred girls from grades seven to thirteen. Sister Helen had to be even stricter. So, I made up my mind that I would have to be on my best behavior. Sister Helen showed me to a room where she wanted me to spend the night in the convent's guest house. Thank God, they didn't want me sleeping in the dormitory alone, before other students arrived. It would have been really scary. I was grateful that she let me stay in the convent.

When it was time for my guardian angel Ananias to leave, my eyes started to feel the burn from acid tears. This was the worst goodbye moment I had ever had. As soon as he announced his leaving, a stream of tears filled my eyes. All the tears I had been holding back for days, since leaving home, were now spilling down. I didn't want him to leave me. I cried a river of tears that refused to drain. I didn't know where the tears were coming from, and I tried to compose myself. I reasoned myself that after all, this man was only a good Samaritan and not my father. But I couldn't stop crying. Ananias tried to lecture me again about the importance of education.

"Don't cry, my child. This is a good school, and you will learn a lot. Education is good. It's in your best interest to stay and learn."

But the tears kept running down my cheeks regardless. When I tried to stop crying, the terrible sobs that took over and shook me were even worse. Sister Marie and Sister Helen also tried their best to console me. Sister Marie ordered her maid to bring me warm milk with sugar, but I couldn't drink it or swallow. And when I tried for the nun's sake, my stomach couldn't keep it down, so I stopped trying. I was a mess!

Eventually, Ananias had to leave. Like a mother trying to separate herself from her toddler on the first day of daycare, he had to turn away and leave me there without looking back. He had to return to his evangelizing job. He had a mission in life, so he couldn't just stay there and babysit me. The two nuns assured him that I would be fine.

"Don't worry, Pastor. Once other students start coming, she will adjust," Sister Marie told Ananias, and Sister Helen nodded in confirmation. Seemingly shocked as well, Pastor Ananias gathered his courage and left me there with the nuns. I cried until I was dehydrated.

Later that evening, three seventh graders came to spend the night. Then, because we were four, the nuns let us sleep in the dormitory where seventh graders would be sleeping. I was ecstatic! This was a school after all, and not just a nun's place? Other kids would come here to study? All my tears dried away, and all my anxiety vanished. They were replaced by a sense of relief and hope.

We went into the dormitory to make our beds, but the other girls did not know how. I am proud to say I was the savvier one. Those girls were accompanied by their dads, of course—lucky them. One girl's dad helped her make her bed. First, he put the blanket on the bed and then the sheets on top. But this was not a warm region, so I didn't think he did it on purpose. The girl was seemingly embarrassed, but out of respect, she didn't tell her dad he had made the bed upside down. I was envious that at least her dad was with her and trying to help her get settled in a boarding school.

At my grandparents' house, I had been trained in making beds by Melanie, Uncle Apollinaire's wife. They had a modern bed, with a mattress and sheets, of course. She had taught me how to make a bed, insisting that I had to know for when I would have a husband. It became my job to make their bed every day because when my uncle was away, I shared their bed with Melanie. But I was kicked out whenever my uncle came home for vacations; then I shared my bed with Barenga instead. We slept on the floor where we laid thick grass for cushioning, and laid covers on top. That was our bed. But as soon as my uncle left to go back to his military job, I slept on their modern bed with Melanie.

As at any good school for girls only, the nuns trained us how to make our beds properly. They also taught us good manners, including good hygiene. They taught us about menstruation, and how to wear feminine pads for those of us who didn't know yet. This was definitely a fine girls' school!

It was during that year in seventh grade that I got my first period. This was not good news for me. I was away from my family for the first time, and from my big sisters who already knew about getting your period. I was also away from my adopted aunt Barenga, who had taught me so much about a girl becoming a woman after she got her first period. As far as I was concerned, sex education had mostly been taught by Barenga. She taught me much of what I knew until further details were acquired in high school from friends and biology classes (particularly the chapter on human reproduction). Barenga was the one who informed me about girls menstruating and why it happened. She called it *"kuja mu kwezi"* ("going into the moon") because menstruations happen once a month, and the months were counted by full moons, the equivalent of a lunar calendar. Barenga used to tell me, "At around twelve years old, you may see blood come out of your girly parts."

"Why?" I would inquire with worried eyes at the mention of blood.

"Because God created a girl to become a woman, and to bear children," she would say.

But I couldn't make the connection between having children and the bleeding part. Then she would go on to say, "Bleeding each month is a way of preparing a girl for womanhood."

Barenga taught me more than my own mother did on the subject. As a matter of fact, my mother never taught me anything about sex. Sex education wasn't part of how parents raised their children. It was a taboo subject, and we kids kept to ourselves whatever information we had about sex. However, by the time I went to live with my parents, I knew a lot, thanks to Barenga. For a woman who never went to school, she was awfully smart.

It would have been nice if my becoming a woman could have happened when I was home with my family. But, no.... I had to be far away! I didn't tell anyone at school; I didn't really want anyone to know. Even though I knew that this day would eventually come, I still felt like it was a bad thing having my period. It felt as if I had done something wrong or committed a sin. This was because, in my culture, having your period had a certain stigma to it. In the Burundian traditions, like when my mother was growing up in the 1940s, when a girl had her period, she was not allowed to go outside. She was forced to stay indoors until her period ended. The traditions made it seem like she was dirty or had some impurity.

When I had my first period, I didn't have money to buy real feminine pads like Kotex, which was the brand the rich girls used. I resorted to using toilet paper as a pad. I would pull off a long sheet of toilet paper and roll it, making sure it was heavily padded enough, imitating the shape of a real feminine pad. And I would wear it as a pad to block the blood. But it was the worst pad ever! After a while, it would be soaked and roll out of my underwear, and go up my back. Then, without my knowledge, it would drop on the ground when I was walking. That was the most embarrassing thing ever! When I noticed it had dropped, I would just keep walking, pretending it wasn't mine, because I didn't want anyone to know it was.

And it wasn't just me using toilet paper as a pad. Many other, less-than-fortunate girls used it, and it was the same. You would just see some bloody, dried-out toilet paper dropped on the ground and pretend you didn't see it. In eighth grade, I started using real pads that were available in stores. I had never seen tampons, nor was I impressed when I saw them for the first time in North America.

Today, in many African countries, there are still girls who drop out of school to deal with menstruations. Some families still stigmatize having a period, and many girls in developing countries, especially in the villages don't have access to feminine pads, so they resort to staying home. In many cases, this is one of the reasons girls in those villages end up dropping out of school.

My first night in the boarding school, I slept like a baby. Let's face it; I was probably exhausted from all that crying. It would be the first of my many happy nights, and no more crying, until the first Christmas break, when I went home for the holidays.

CHAPTER 8

Christmas Break

MY FIRST CHRISTMAS BREAK in high school started in mid-December. The plan was that my family would send me money for the transportation fare, using a postal money order, so I could go back and visit them. At the lycée, there was a routine: On the Friday preceding the return home for the holiday was a money orders day. All the students were gathered in front of their dormitories, and names were called for those who got money orders.

That Friday, when the nun in charge called names, my name didn't get called. I hoped to be next, or next, or maybe next...but no! Almost every kid in seventh grade got a money order except me. I didn't cry. Oh, no, I was a big girl now. But mostly, I didn't cry because I kept expecting money for some reason, without knowing who was going to be my next good Samaritan. Friday afternoon gave way to Saturday morning, and my money order still hadn't come. All the students were to leave on Saturday around 10 a.m., so I started to fear the worst. Where was I going to be when everybody would climb the school pickup to go home? I didn't have any idea. My mind raced with possibilities, but I refused to consider that I wouldn't be going home.

On Saturday, when it was almost time for students to leave school, Sister Helen came to my dorm and called me. Whew! My money had come after all! I finally had a return home transportation ticket for Christmas vacation like the other kids. Two thousand Burundi francs (less than one US dollar today) was wealth to me at that time, although today it would buy almost nothing. I checked the sender section on the money order to find out who had sent me the money. Who else than my beloved Uncle Vincent? It was the happiest moment of my life. I, too, was going home to see my family. It seemed as if God had worked out some wonders again. Don't you think? My parents never could have afforded a bus ticket to bring me home for the holidays and send me back to school in only two weeks.

The plan was to go from my school, the Lycée of Gisanze, to Bujumbura. Once in Bujumbura, I would take another bus to Vugizo, my hometown. I was certainly looking forward to going home to show off how many inches taller I had grown, and how much weight I had gained. Yeah, believe me, I wanted to gain weight back then! Except for my behind, the rest of my body was small.

Since the morning the holidays started, wealthy parents who had cars had been coming to pick up their kids. Some students in the senior grades (twelve and thirteen) who had wealthy boyfriends with cars were picked up as well. But the vast majority of us paid for our own transportation, which consisted of the school pickup, courtesy of the lycée, packing as many students aboard as it could. The school pickup drove students and dropped them off at a junction road on the outskirts between the provinces of Muyinga and Kirundo, where the traffic flowed more frequently. Priority was given to those who lived the farthest from the school, which meant all the students from farther south in the province of Bururi (which included the now province of Makamba, where I came from). From that junction, students then took whatever had wheels to Ngozi city center. Once in Ngozi, we rushed to climb on the minibuses, the famous *Hiaces* to Bujumbura. After Bujumbura, I still had to take connecting transportation to Vugizo to get home.

I was so excited to ride along with other students and not miss any of the fun. I was so ready for any mischief that would come my way on that school pickup. The girls' chanting had already begun. As I started climbing into the back of the school pickup, I saw Pastor Ananias approaching on his bicycle. *The bicycle?* Oh, God, not the bicycle again! I panicked. Why was he here? What was the problem? Didn't he get the memo that this was the happiest, wildest moment in my youth? I was going home after three months of absence to see my family.

Pastor Ananias approached the school pickup and spoke to one of the teachers, Mr. Menard, who taught in the upper grades and happened to be from my hometown. I watched the two men speak in a low tone, but my instincts had already told me what they were talking about. Then I heard Pastor Ananias telling Mr. Menard, "I've come to take the child to my home in Muyinga, to spend the Christmas holidays with me. She is too young to travel home and back to school alone." My heart sank.

Mr. Menard approached the back of the pickup where the students were piled up, ready to go home. He looked at me and said, "Seconde, step down. Pastor Ananias has come to take you to his house for the Christmas break."

Without even thinking, I said, "No!" Then before I could blink, my eyes started spilling burning tears. Between my tears and a broken voice, I told Ananias, "I received the transportation ticket from my uncle, and he is expecting me to go home and I want to go home." Ananias reasoned with me for some time, until the Toyota pickup was about to leave without me.

"My friends are going home. Why not me?" I threw a big seventh-grade tantrum. Then both men realized how upset I was, and Mr. Menard persuaded the pastor to let me go home, offering to chaperone me. Convinced that I would be in Mr. Menard's good hands, Pastor Ananias let me go home. All my friends were happy for me as I climbed back in the pickup. We left and didn't waste any time singing our wildest songs. I didn't know where those girls had learned all those songs. The songs were filled with words we wouldn't necessarily say in front of our parents.

As we hurried to board the crowded minibuses in Ngozi's city center, Mr. Menard made sure I was still among the crowd. We took our bus to Bujumbura, where we arrived in the night. Again, when I saw it from the upper hills of Ijenda when approaching the capital, Bujumbura glowed. My heart soared with pride for my country's beautiful city of light. Although I could have gone to dad's second cousin's house to spend the night, I didn't know how to get there, and it was late at night. So Mr. Menard decided I would go with him to spend the night where he was going.

We went to a poor neighborhood that had squalid houses, basically a slum. I didn't sleep well; my night was aggravated by the heat and mosquito bites. But I kept my spirits up because I knew that the next day, I would see my family. I couldn't wait for the day to come.

The next day, Mr. Menard came to wake me up at six in the morning. We went to the central market, where we took the bus from Bujumbura to my hometown. The bus ride had many stops in different cities along the way and was long and bumpy to boot. It took me the whole day to get home.

My parents and siblings were happy to see me. And yes, they confirmed that I had grown taller, indeed. In our immediate family, we were not meant to be tall, so I was doing my part as best I could. Two weeks went by fast, but it was the best vacation ever spent with my family. My siblings said my accent had changed yet again. They said I now spoke with a Kinyarwanda (Rwandan language) accent. Because of my school's proximity to Rwanda, a lot of Rwandan students were at the school, and four of the nuns who ran the school, as well as some of the teachers, were Rwandans. So, it is possible my accent had really changed. After my two weeks' holiday ended, going back to school presented other challenges I hadn't foreseen.

I left home on the day Christmas break ended to go to Bujumbura. That part presented no problems. The next day, I took the bus to Ngozi's city center. I spent the night at the home of Uncle Vincent's friend, a military officer whom my uncle had asked to help me in Ngozi. The plan was that my uncle's friend would put me on the bus to Muyinga the next day. There was no straight transportation to Gisanze, the remote village where my school was located. That's why the school had arranged to pick students up at a junction road at an intersection between the road to Gisanze and the road to the center of the Muyinga province. This arrangement ran only on the first day of school. If you were not there on that specific day, and at a specific time, the school pickup would never see you, and you would never meet your school pickup either. I missed it because I went to the pickup location on the second day of school. The day I was supposed to get on the school pickup was the one I spent in Ngozi.

The army officer who housed me in Ngozi went to the market with me the next morning. He put me on the bus to Muyinga with the understanding that I would have to get off at the intersection, where I should have met the school pickup the previous day. I knew I would not be meeting any school pickup there, so I had to walk to school from that intersection. It was at least ten miles, but nothing to worry about. I was used to walking since primary school. I don't know exactly what time I got there, but it was early afternoon, so I was not afraid that I would have to walk in the night. I didn't have any heavy bags, only my little bag of a few belongings and my tuition money that Uncle Vincent had given me for the second trimester. So, I had to hold on tight to this money and not lose it.

After I got off the bus to Muyinga at the right intersection, I started walking along the one road to the school. The road was surrounded by high bushes and trees. But I didn't have the luxury of thinking scary thoughts because I had to walk fast. On my way to school, I met people going about their daily business, but each man I met carried a machete in his hand. Now, a machete is a cutting tool, so I thought maybe they were going to cut trees or grass or whatever.

But because in 1972, during the civil war in Burundi, machetes were used to kill Tutsis, I didn't feel safe meeting these people carrying machetes. In addition, Muyinga, the province where my school was located, was one of the most affected by the wars of 1972 and 1973, and was a Hutu majority province. Furthermore, I remembered the myths about there being people in that region who turned into werewolves after sunset. I consider this a myth now, but it was a scary myth for a seventh grader; life is too sweet to be eaten by werewolves.

Perhaps because of my fear of being killed by those machete holders, or eaten in case they turned into werewolves, I must have released my mighty grip on the handkerchief in which I had wrapped my tuition money. My total wealth consisted of the tuition money, and a little extra cash for my living expenses for the second trimester, all tied up in a pretty white hanky I had bought for that purpose. Now it was gone! But I couldn't walk back to look for it, could I? After walking for a while, I stopped worrying that someone was going to eat me. I wasn't that good, or chubby. I then realized for real that I had lost my money.

"My money—the money Uncle Vincent gave me! Oh, my God. I lost my tuition money!" I freaked out for a few seconds, and then I tried to calm myself down. "Stay calm, stay calm." And miraculously, I did calm down. I usually cried in every other situation, but I never cried in a difficult situation like this.

I turned and started going back the way I had come, looking on the ground to try to see where I had dropped my money. I didn't care anymore about meeting bad guys because I had lost my tuition money. I had to find it. I kept walking faster, looking on the ground with all the mighty vision I had been given, trying to use my intuition to locate where I might have loosened my grip and dropped the money. I tried to walk as fast as I could, almost jogging.

After twenty minutes or so of walking back, I saw a man holding a machete in his hand, walking in my direction. Immediately, I turned back, this time walking toward the school where I was supposed to be going in the first place. I gave up on the money because the man kept making signs to me, like a sign language. He was either going to eat me, or kill me, or both. I was sure of it. My thoughts raced and I started rushing, speeding up my pace, so he wouldn't reach me. The faster I walked, the faster he walked, and he continued signaling to me as I looked back under my armpits. He was faster than me, and I was starting to feel exhausted. When he was a couple of feet away from me, he finally spoke.

"Child, did you lose something?" he asked me.

"Yes!" I blurted out, feeling jumpy.

"What was it?" he inquired.

"I lost my school money. I am going to school at the Lycée of Gisanze and I lost my school fees...."

I was ready to give every detail of my life to this stranger if he would listen and help me find my school money.

"Where did you put it?" he asked.

"I wrapped it in a small white handkerchief, and—" I wanted to volunteer the rest of the details, but he interrupted me and asked,

"Did it look like this?" He showed me the little hanky.

"Yes! Oh, my God, yes, that's my money!" I said with a trembling voice, longing for a good emotional release. But I was afraid the stranger might notice how scared I was, decide to eat me instead, and take my money after all. So, I decided to sound grown up. He handed me the handkerchief still wrapped. I didn't even open it to see whether, indeed, my money was still there or to count it. I was just grateful my hanky was still wrapped and white.

"Thank you, thank you, thank you so very much!" I said to the stranger. Before he left to continue his day, I braced myself and mumbled, "I would love to give you some of the money to thank you, but it's for the school tuition." (Great, now I sounded too cheap).

Although I itched with guilt for not giving him a monetary reward, there was no way for me to do so without falling short on the tuition.

"No child, you don't need to give me anything. Just rush and get to school before sunset," he said and left.

Aha, sunset! That woke me up from my dream because it felt so surreal that someone was being so kind toward a vulnerable kid, in the middle of nowhere. I thanked him again, but I felt my words were not enough to express my gratitude. He went on his way. What a good angel! I am sure God has blessed him manyfold, and I am so thankful.

When I arrived at school late that evening, the classes had already been dismissed. I met some girls, walking around the school's neighborhood, taking in the evening breeze. The wind was quiet; the sky was blue. I had missed my first day of class, but I had gained so much more on this journey. I gained the confidence of bringing myself to school under God's watchful eye. And more importantly, I gained confidence in humanity. I felt there were still good people in the world, no matter how they looked or what ethnicity, tribe, race, political affiliation, or religion they belonged to. And to this day, I try to remember not to put people in boxes, but to assess individual behaviors and not judge them because of the group they belong to.

After Uncle Vincent heard about the ordeal I had gone through, he decided that for Easter break, I would not go home. He sent me the bus fare to go to Bujumbura only, and spend the two weeks of the Easter holidays at my dad's second cousin's house. I wasn't happy about not seeing my parents and siblings during the Easter holidays, and not being checked out to see whether I had grown another quarter of an inch, but two weeks in the big city of Bujumbura was better than the bicycle ride to the pastor's house. Not that I didn't appreciate the pastor's kindness, but there were no kids to play with at his house. He lived with another evangelist, and I had no one to talk to. They went preaching most of the day and prayed almost all night long. Regardless, I truly thank Ananias; he was there for me during one of the important events in my youth, more than my own father.

After that first year of high school, Uncle Vincent arranged to transfer me to another high school nearer to home, but far enough that it took me two whole days to walk there. There wasn't any high school in my province of Makamba at that time, let alone in my hometown.

I was relieved, but also disappointed by the transfer. First, I would not see again all the friends I had made in seventh grade. And second, even though it was an ordeal to go to the Lycée of Gisanze, at least I took transportation—something moving on wheels. But at the new school, I would be walking my butt off every time I went to school or came home. It was a very exhausting trip, all on foot.

CHAPTER 9

A New School

AFTER SEVENTH GRADE, I started eighth grade at a new school called Lycée of Rubanga, located in the province of Bururi (in southern Burundi). The new adventure at the new school was that I now had to travel on foot the whole way. Not just for a few hours like I did in primary school, not for a day, but for two whole days. I traveled with a couple of other less-than-fortunate students who walked to high school. One of them was a girl named Mathilda who was in the tenth grade and lived across the valley from our house. As soon as my mother learned about my school transfer, she appointed Mathilda to look out for me when we walked to school, like a kind of big sister.

Whenever school began, Mathilda and I left two days early to get to school on time. On the departure day, my oldest sister Eugenie woke me up at 4 a.m., after she had packed my lunch and readied my breakfast. My mother would rush me, saying, "Eat your breakfast fast!" But I couldn't eat that early. After mom had irritated me enough with her nagging, I would just give up eating breakfast altogether. I wished I could go back to sleep, but I had to go to school.

My mother always accompanied me to Mathilda's house to make sure I wouldn't be alone when crossing the valley on the way to her house. I remember one time we got to Mathilda's house after she had left. My mom almost had a heart attack, she was so distressed. She accompanied me for a couple of miles to make sure I could catch up with Mathilda. I was more worried about my mom having to walk alone all the way back home. Fortunately, Mathilda had stopped and was waiting for me.

The first day of my journey to the new school, I set out in the early morning and walked past the big Mount Inanzegwe, a mountain of more than 7,000 feet elevation— a mini-Everest of some sort. Not only was Mount Inanzegwe a high mountain to climb, but its rocks and cumbersome stones made it hard to walk. I was always beyond exhaustion when we finally arrived at the peak of the mountain, only to realize that descending was as hard as climbing. People in the Western world, like in the United States, climb mountains for fun, as an adventure. For me, climbing Mount Inanzegwe was the only way to reach school. Many times, on that mountain, I thought about dropping out of high school. But something inside my heart said, *No. You must do this. You don't have the luxury of feeling sorry for yourself, Seconde. You are one of the privileged ones who get to attend high school.* And so, I pressed on, climbed, and hiked the endless mountain.

At sunset, Mathilda and I decided we needed a place to sleep for the night and wait for the next day. So, we went to spend the night at people's houses—people we didn't even know. Whatever house was nearby was our main target. We would just go to someone's house and say, "Hello, anybody home? We are students going to the Lycée of Rubanga, and we need a place to spend the night." Mathilda usually did the talking. No family ever refused to house us for the night in my entire six years of going to that school. People were always very kind and understanding. They treated us as special guests for the night. After a while, we started spotting a good family that would feed us well—a mix of rice and beans with palm butter, and we stuck with that family.

Every new school year and during the holidays, that family would kind of expect us. And it wasn't just Mathilda and me. After we had walked several miles, we met with other students of various grades. Together, we spent the night with our favorite host. Unlike my former school, Lycée of Rubanga was a gender-mixed school, so there were boys and girls. After we had joined the others, I enjoyed having older students help me carry my luggage, and walk at my slow pace, when I was tired and sweating salt. I couldn't wait to have some place to sleep for the night, and I would sleep like a rock without moving any part of my little body.

The next morning, which always came fast, we had to get up as early as possible since it would be our arrival day at school. I usually couldn't walk. My feet were so swollen that I had to limp. However, after a couple of miles walking, I had no other choice than to press on my feet to carry me to school. The second day was a little better than the first. There was no more mini-Everest to climb, only small hills and valleys, and usually a pleasant landscape to look at. Depending on how fast we were, the final leg of this trip usually took us between seven and eight hours.

Again, why all this going to school when it was so painful? By then, my parents, even my father, had warmed up to the idea that I had to continue school. They had seen no potential in my farming skills, and they had decided that maybe, just maybe, one day, in addition to marrying someone important, I could be someone important myself. My mother was doing the best she could to help raise money for our school needs. She saved up a little money from selling grains from our crops at the market in the summer. She then gave my brothers and me some money to buy school supplies, such as notebooks, pens, pencils, toiletries, and other little things we needed for school so that Uncle Vincent only needed to give us the tuition money.

When we finally got to school, we were excited to see the other students, especially our friends, and hear all they had to say about what had happened over the summer vacations. Some students who came from well-to-do families reported having traveled to the city of Bujumbura, or told stories of where they went to foreign countries for tourism. Not only did I not have anything special to report, but I was always too tired to enjoy the reunion. My feet were swollen for the entire week. Sometimes, Mathilda came to my dorm to see how I was doing, and she massaged my feet using a piece of cloth dampened in lukewarm water she got from the school kitchen. She took good care of me, just like my mother had asked her to do.

After the first week, I felt better. I loved school. I loved learning, but not studying. My natural strengths were in literature and social studies, but these seemed to be my least favorite subjects. So, I didn't study much, only getting by with what the teacher had taught during the class. But I took math and the sciences seriously. Because one of my brothers was a nerd in math and the sciences, I wanted to show him that I, too, a girl, could do well in those subjects. Physics and chemistry were very tough classes, but as I grew older, I got decent grades, although never high enough to guarantee me a placement in a scientific section in the upper grades.

After tenth grade, we had to be placed in senior high (grades eleven to thirteen), according to what we wanted to be when we grew up. Those who were strong in math and the sciences were placed in the scientific sections—the future Einsteins! My brother Cyriaque was one of those, but at a separate lycée, thank God. The idea of attending the same high school with him would have been terrifying. He was so book smart and too serious to enjoy the teenage life. I didn't want him yelling at me if I didn't get good grades in math or the sciences. But there was an unspoken responsibility on his part toward me. He wanted me to excel in those subjects so I would wind up in a scientific major and follow in his footsteps. Soft subjects such as literature or social studies were kind of undervalued in Burundi.

I wasn't that bad in math, but I wasn't as nerdy as my brother. Even then, it was still thought that girls would be better off with social skills because they were expected to marry someone important. They didn't really need math skills or big degrees. As long as girls knew how to count money, supervise good housekeeping, and entertain social gatherings, they were fine. There was also the stereotype that if a woman was too smart, men would be intimidated, which would make it hard for the woman to find a husband. So, educating a girl was like a business trying to increase its shareholders' value. The father could then expect two cows instead of one for his daughter's dowry, if she was educated just enough, but not too much. Thus, high school diplomas qualified women to get married to high-ranking politicians, military officers, and even uneducated millionaires.

Yes, I admit, one of my objectives in going to high school was to find an educated husband. I had a little voice in my head telling me not to settle for the farming, cooking and cleaning. By all means, I wanted to avoid having to live my mother's life. I wanted to have choices my mom never had her entire life. Therefore, it was a good fortune that my innate knowledge in literature and languages afforded me the opportunity to continue in the upper grades that would qualify me to go to the university. That meant I needed to focus more on social studies, such as world history and geography, as well as more French literature classes and a little English.

After tenth grade, my placement in the literature major was in part due to my French literature teacher, Mr. Freddy. He was adamant that I would study literature and go on to the university. I had decided that after tenth grade, I wanted to study nursing. I wanted to attend nursing school because it was well known for its good food. The students who went there reported being well-fed and well-tended. The Lycée of Rubanga fed us so poorly that I was often sick. I had decided that after tenth grade, I would go to nursing school, so I would be well fed and maybe grow another couple of inches.

However, because I was part of the school's theatrical team, Mr. Freddy refused to let me go to the nursing high school for my high school senior years. After tenth grade, the school-teacher committee had a say in recommending the placement of its students. And because of my involvement in the school plays, Mr. Freddy wanted to keep me at the school for my upper grades. By staying at the Lycée of Rubanga, I was guaranteed to go to the university, provided I passed the national exam in the last year of high school, of course.

I always played the lead role in the school plays, which had become popular. Mr. Freddy was the head of the school's theatrical productions, which he chose and directed. We used to take our school plays on tour (yes, just like on Broadway!) to the other schools in the province of Bururi, and we made good money for the school.

Mr. Freddy saw some potential in me that I didn't even know I had. I had a good French pronunciation, so Mr. Freddy always chose me for the lead female character in every play. I loved it! Finally, someone was paying attention to me and believing in me. In addition, I had a good memory, so my brain would remember my lines the first time I read the script.

My acting career resulted from my studying both French and African literature. I liked being on stage during plays. It was both scary and exhilarating, especially if the plays were good enough to provoke emotions. My character was always somehow good, always a person of integrity, and, of course, I was some fairy-tale princess facing cultural conflicts between modern and old times, new and old generations, especially in the African literature. It was a treat.

I liked being in some of the African storytellers' plays. They wrote about events their people had lived through, such as the slavery, colonial, and post-colonial eras. They also wrote about conflicts between generations, young versus old, urban versus village. Our school plays attracted the local community, and especially, teachers and students from the Lycée of Matana, a boys-only high school. They came to watch our plays on Saturday nights in the big refectory that we converted into a theatre with mounted tables and chairs and surrounded with huge drapes hanging from the ceiling. If you didn't know better, you would think it was a real stage. That refectory was a multipurpose room. We used it as a dining hall, then on Saturdays after dinner, we transformed it into a dancing hall, and when we had plays, it became a theatre hall.

My senior high school years went by fast because I was having fun. Although I was a shy girl, when on stage, I just lived in the moment and forgot all about my timidity. I thank Mr. Freddy for the gift of validation.

• • •

In my entire thirteen years of high school education, there wasn't a moment when I could relax about the school fees. I always had the same anxiety that my brothers and I would not have school money and might miss the year. I was also feeling guilty about how we imposed on Uncle Vincent to pay for our schooling. Sometimes, we didn't receive the money until two days before school began. And we didn't have summer jobs where we could earn a little money. The school system had no student-paid jobs; we only worked for our families. We would have worked our butts off if there were such opportunities.

Although Uncle Vincent always paid our tuition, and my father had come to rely on his brother's kindness, my brothers and I viewed it as imposing on our uncle and even begging. We were always mad at our father for never providing for our schooling needs.

One time, Uncle Vincent did not send us our school money. We had been waiting for him to send it, but we still didn't have it two days before school started. We didn't know what to do. So, Emmanuel, Cyriaque, and I packed our bags and went to see Uncle Vincent where he worked as an officer at a military base in Bururi. We walked from home to where he lived, which took more than ten hours, but I loved it for once. It made me closer to my two older brothers. I felt the tuition issue was our shared struggle, and we made an unspoken pact to succeed in school. We were the chosen ones, the lucky ones to attend high school, when so many kids our age couldn't get past sixth grade, and many others didn't even get a chance to start primary school.

Often, our neighbors scolded their children to make them succeed in school, referring to us as role model students in our village. One kid's father always scolded him by saying, "Look at Seconde and her brothers. Why can't you be like them? What do they have that you don't?" As a matter of fact, most of the kids who failed in school had fathers who could afford to pay their tuition and were supportive. Even in my elementary school, some kids had parents who hired private tutors for them, but they weren't necessarily the brightest. They took education for granted because if they didn't pass, their parents or someone in their families could afford to pay fat bribes for them to advance, or repeat the grade as many times as they needed. Not every kid had a chance to repeat the grade more than twice. Usually after two times, you were expelled from school, and that was the end of your education, if you didn't have rich parents.

When we arrived at Uncle Vincent's house, he wasn't expecting us, but he welcomed us anyway. Even though I am sure he instantly knew the motive of our visit, he asked us:

"Why are you here? Shouldn't you be going to your respective schools?"

My brother Cyriaque took the lead by answering, "We don't have tuition money." I could hear his voice shaking in anger, as if to say, "Why would you even ask that question, Uncle?"

"Who am I? Your father? Shouldn't you discuss tuition money with your father?" replied Uncle Vincent, letting us have it for once, but he was too kind to mean it.

Again, my poor brother Cyriaque answered for all of us, and said, "Our father always says he has no money for our tuition, and he cannot afford to send us to high school."

Emmanuel and I just kept quiet, not knowing how we would pull it off this time. Uncle Vincent was only telling us he was getting tired of our financial dependency on him, but he had no way out. My father felt entitled to his younger brother's money. It was how the system worked, and still works today. Those who are well off in the family have to pay the price. Everyone understands that and comes to expect it.

My uncle was paying our tuition as a service to his extended family. He knew if we did well in school and graduated, we would be the next good Samaritans for our extended family. What I loved about my uncle was that he didn't just give us money for tuition and then forget about us. He expected us to do well in school. He had said time and again, "If you fail a grade, and have to repeat it, don't count on me to pay twice for the same grade." As a matter of fact, if we boasted that we had ranked second place in a trimester, he would ask us, "What prevented you from being the first in your class?" and he expected it the next trimester.

My brothers and I did well in high school, and I was glad someone demanded hard work from me in school. To my father, school was just a way to escape home chores, but to Uncle Vincent, we were in school for a noble purpose. He was the pioneer of education in my family.

The last year of my high school education, we had to pass another national exam that helped determine who could go to the university. I got the required passing score, but not high enough to guarantee me a scholarship that would allow me to study abroad. After grade thirteen, it was every student's dream to get a scholarship to study abroad. But only a few select students did. If your grade point average was extra high, some scholarships were available from some Western organizations or countries, as part of the international aid to Burundi. Many were from our previous colonizer, Belgium. Other scholarships were from China and other European countries. Several other coveted foreign-aid scholarships existed, but you had to be the son or daughter of an influential person in the country to get one, or your parents needed to pay a fat bribe. Not only was I not the daughter of an influential person, but my parents couldn't afford to pay a bribe of any amount, so I had to rely on my hard work in school.

In the summer of 1987, I graduated from high school. Hallelujah! Since I had passed the national test that qualified me for university admission, I knew better days were ahead of me, and I was so ready for my wonder years to begin.

CHAPTER 10

University Initiation

IN THE FALL OF 1987, I was a university freshman. Most high school graduates who had passed the national exam entered the one and only university we had at the time—the University of Burundi. I wasn't going to whine about not studying abroad because I had achieved beyond my wildest expectations.

I was placed in arts and humanities despite my dislike of these two fields. The Ministry of Education had disregarded my choice to attend the school of journalism. Journalism was my first choice because I wanted to be a French TV news anchor. I was always mesmerized by journalists who read the news in French on television. With my good pronunciation, I was certain I could be just like them. However, the Ministry of Education enrolled me in arts and humanities instead, even though it was my third choice. Had I been a math nerd like my brother Cyriaque, I would have studied economics like he had asked me to.

In Burundi, economics was and still is highly regarded as a field of study because it helps one be considered for high-paying jobs. Economists could easily find good jobs in banks and the government, and they were more eligible for international organizations such as the World Bank or the International Monetary Fund. Arts and humanities graduates were mostly guaranteed a teaching job, usually in a remote area, for the rest of their lives. Teaching in Burundi is the most underpaid and under-promoted job. With such a degree, opportunities don't knock on one's door.

My high school trauma being over, I now had a shot at a better life. At the university, I would start wearing real shoes, not just the click-clack flip-flops I had worn all high school long. No problem—I could afford shoes and clothes, because in addition to housing the students and feeding them for free, the University of Burundi gave us an allowance. Each month, those of us who lived on campus got around 3,000 Burundi francs (roughly one US dollar today), but at that time, it was worth much more than it is nowadays. And those who chose to live outside of the campus received even higher monetary allowances. I had no other bills to pay, so each month, I sent some money to my mother, and once in a while, I sent money to my two younger siblings, Teresa and Francis, who were still in high school. I was rich, people!

The first couple of months at the University of Burundi were torturous if you were a spoiled brat, and my family had awarded me that title long ago. The first few weeks, all the freshmen had to go through something called *initiation*. This was a ritual performed mostly by the university sophomores who were doing to the new students what had been done to them the previous year, when they were freshmen themselves. They started their session of initiation early in September, when it was time for registration at the main campus located in the capital city of Bujumbura.

I remember my first initiation when I went to register. I was staying again at dad's second cousin's house where I had spent my Easter holiday in seventh grade. He seemed to be the only relative living in the capital at that time. On registration day, I walked to the registrar's office from his house, only three miles away. I had been told that on registration day, I would encounter the *"poil"* (pronounced: pwal), meaning the "initiated." You could only be a *"poil"* if you had already gone through the initiation. The initiation itself was called *"baptême"* (French for baptism). I don't recall my captor's name, but I remember being approached by a young man. (Boys seemed to enjoy initiating girls.) He asked me a couple of smart questions typically asked of the *"puants."* Those enduring the initiation rites were called *puants*, literally meaning "stinky." That's right, we freshmen were told that we stank. The *"poils"* called themselves, "the omnipotent, omnipresent, and omniscient," as if they were gods. They said we, the stinky freshmen, had some type of bug that we needed to get out of our systems. We were also called "blue," another term used to describe our naiveté.

Coming from high schools all over the country to the University of Burundi, most freshmen didn't know what they were stepping into. Even some parents were freaked out when their kids went to the university. Not that my parents were freaked out; by then, they had admitted my potential to become somebody.

After answering my initiator's questions, I was released to go register, but he promised me he would still be there when I returned from the registrar's office. I panicked. I anticipated humiliation on the *Boulevard du 28 Novembre*, a road located a couple of feet from the university, where the *poils* waited for freshmen to introduce them to the initiation rites during registration. That boulevard was at a U-turn road, where the traffic was very busy, so it provided a treat for passersby to enjoy some humor while watching the initiation scene. But it was the worst nightmare for us, the "stinky." It was even worse if somebody you knew saw you being humiliated. Fortunately, during my entire initiation time, no one outside the university community saw me performing the rituals.

I survived that first day of initiation because when I came out of the registrar's office, all *poils* had gone to lunch. I went home as fast as I could before they could come back. But the initiation was only postponed until university classes began.

When the classes started, the initiation was only performed during recess, or during lunch and dinner times. That's when our inner strengths were put to the test. If you weren't up to the torture of being initiated, you couldn't eat. And even if you ate, it was with such anxiety. Some girls just gave up going to the dining hall altogether and cooked on their portable stoves in their campus dorm rooms. Others, who had relatives nearby, went to their houses for meals. I didn't have a close relative nearby with whom I felt comfortable enough to have my meals. Even if I had, I wouldn't want to impose or take advantage of my relative just because I was afraid of being "baptized."

So, I made up my mind. I decided that whatever initiation torture there would be, I would endure it. This was a very smart move on my part because the more I did, whatever the day's rituals were, the more I got the hang of it, and the less I was anguished by the whole initiation process. I decided the only way to get through the initiation was to go through it, head on. BAM!

The rituals were nothing traumatic if you were brave. Mostly, the *poils* wanted the freshmen to sing loudly some lyrics containing names of female and male private parts. We had to perform those lyrics in front of other students and anyone who happened to pass by. Saying the private body parts in French was somehow bearable. But to say those words in the Kirundi language, and come up with ten synonyms for each private part, was very humiliating! I would just shyly whisper the words, and then my initiator would say:

"*Puante*, repeat more loudly, so every *poil* can hear you. Go on, say it louder!"

I would then repeat just as softly, only to make my initiator more upset, and be ordered to repeat it ten times louder, under the cackling laughs of those watching. After saying those words time and again, I felt dirty and truly needed a shower!

When my initiator felt satisfied that I had been humiliated enough, he set me free to go and eat. I was always caught when going to the dining hall. I had to eat, you know. The next day, the *poils* would see me again and make sure I endured the same rituals as the day before. Depending on the special initiation menu of the day, I would do whatever they asked, so I could get my meal. After a couple of days seeing me coming and going, the *poils* laughed at me. One guy said, "*Puante*, you're back? Why aren't you frightened like the other girls who go eat at their aunties' houses? Huh? Oh, wait! You have no auntie in the city?" he said to me, mockingly, and then rubbed his beard he had grown for the occasion. That hurt my feelings because I wished I had an auntie in the city, or some immediate family I could count on to hide me during the initiation time. But my immediate family lived in my hometown, and I only had distant relatives in the capital. I had to be strong and pass this initiation, if I wanted to stay in school. I had come a long way, baby, and no initiation was going to stop me from getting a higher education.

I continued to go through the initiation and get my three meals a day at the dining hall. After a week or so, I had two nicknames. One was *Daring Freshman* and the other was *Brave Puante*, because I didn't chicken out during the initiation. That earned me respect from the *poils* and the admiration of the *puants*—the stinky!

Some of my peers would ask me, "Seconde, how do you do it? How come you're not afraid of the *poils?*"

"Of course, I'm afraid. But I need my three meals, girlfriends." I would tell my freshmen mates.

In less than two weeks, the *poils* had stopped harassing me, and I was set free. If an unknowing *poil* tried to stop me, I would hear another one say, "Let her go." Yes! I was happy to have my freedom back.

Those who tried to hide to avoid the initiation were severely punished if they were apprehended. They were dipped in a muddy ditch the *poils* called *Muchuti River*, which served as a drain located in front of the main campus restaurant, or put on the ground and covered in dirt, an act the *poils* called "*Guhamba*," "to bury." This, for girls, was the ultimate death sentence, since they didn't want to mess up their clothes and makeup. I was never dipped in the *Muchuti River* or put on the ground. Only reluctant *puants*, those who refused to obey the initiation rules were.

The initiation's wrap-up day was on a Saturday, close to a month after the academic year had started. That was when classes started to heat up and professors to get in the mood for serious teaching, after a three-month vacation. On Saturday afternoon, all the important *poils* lined up all the stinky freshmen. I couldn't contain my amusement at the *poils'* self-importance. Some even wore ties to mark the closing ceremonies. We were ordered to march from the main campus of Mutanga to Ngangara, another campus approximately three miles away, to meet up with the freshmen from other campuses.

When we arrived on the other campus, we were set free. We became *poils* ourselves and could socialize with the other students. It felt like a graduation from *Stinky High* for me. It was a coming of age in its own right. From that time, freshmen earned the right to perform the same initiation rituals the following year to the in-coming freshmen to keep the tradition alive. I never baptized anybody in my entire academic life. Although it was a delight to watch, when it was being done to others, I couldn't torture another soul. I know, sweet me.

Despite its unpleasantness, I think the freshman initiation was needed. It was a rite of passage from high school to university. It opened my eyes and made me a little stronger, so I could face the academic life.

The first year at my campus dorm, I shared a room with another girl who was studying economics. The room was big enough for both of us. Personally, I didn't have a lot of stuff, so it was more than large enough. My roommate Jeanne was a very beautiful girl, but very shy. Men, ranging from university students to professionals tried so hard to get her to go on a date with them, but she always turned them down. That first year, classes were a bit challenging for me, because I wasn't used to the academic way of studying. Taking notes while professors lectured was an art in itself. I failed two classes and had to retake exams for them in September, and fortunately, I passed that time.

My second year, the university had just finished a new building, and all the sophomores were the lucky ones to move into the new rooms. The rooms had been built with some extra-nice features, such as a bathroom inside each room, instead of the shared bathrooms we had the previous year. There was a sink and a mirror above the sink—really cool! We also shared rooms. Roommates were assigned by the university's logistics office.

My roommate and I didn't exactly become BFFs. From the beginning, she built a wall between us that could be read as, "Stay away from me, I'll stay away from you." And it stayed that way for the entire year. She and I weren't of the same ethnic background, which seemed to be the problem. Old wounds between Tutsis and Hutus had been reopened in 1988, when killings occurred in the Northern provinces, especially in Muyinga (where I had spent seventh grade). As a result, university students were very apprehensive about other ethnicities.

No doubt, my roommate and I were playing ethnicity politics without any spoken words. Our non-verbal language said it all. Because she was Hutu and I, Tutsi, we just chose to stay away from each other, only talking when absolutely necessary, such as to clarify what was for lunch for that day, or to complain about it. However, in my heart of hearts, I believed my roommate would never hurt me, and I think she had the same trust in me. My roommate was studying the sciences, and I was studying literature and social sciences. Again, this made for a difficult match. The students in the sciences kind of looked down on us people of literary endeavors, as if we had nothing to learn—nothing new at least. In the science majors, students studied nonstop. We used to joke that they didn't seem to feel the mosquito bites, while we students of literature had boys coming into our rooms to kill the mosquitoes for us.

One time, a male student came into my room, and after a long silence, because he was too shy to ask me out, he started swatting mosquitoes. He got this poor mosquito into his hand and gallantly crushed it, showing off how heroic he could be. I imagined him saying, "You see, girl, if you go out with me, I will take care of ya. I will kill all the mosquitoes in the Bujumbura valley. I will kill all the mosquitoes in the whole tropical world!" Students in sciences studied as if there were no tomorrow, while in literature, we enjoyed life on the campus, discovering each other on a deeper level.

But it was my roommate who had a boyfriend, a serious one, and not me! They were engaged. Whenever her man came to see her in the room we shared, I would get out of the room, not because they forced me to, but because I knew when two consenting adults needed their privacy. I never failed to give her space when her fiancé visited her in our room. I would go into my best friend Beatrice's room instead, to catch up on the latest gossip. Beatrice and I became best friends our second year at the university. Whenever Beatrice's roommate wasn't in the room, I would sneak in and we would talk and giggle, then count our miseries of not having boyfriends. After Beatrice and I finished whining about our lack of a dating life, we would enjoy music on her radio, and sing our hearts out to Paul Young's "Every Time You Go Away."

I know what you're thinking: *You didn't have a boyfriend in college?* That is the same question my kids asked me when they were teenagers. They wanted to know whether I had a boyfriend before meeting their dad. Here is what I told them, "I only had guy friends, not boyfriends." They would roll their eyes and say, "Sure, Mom. You're just saying that because you don't want us to date before marriage." They were...kind of right.

My dating started right on track my junior year at the university. I met a man whom my relatives, who meant well, encouraged to pursue me. And he was a working adult. Because I viewed dating students as a pastime, I played a little hard to get. Given that I was a late bloomer, I didn't want to waste my time with a boy who wasn't a "somebody" yet. I needed a shortcut in life for once. I wanted a man who would make me his wife.

Many girls who were juniors and seniors were married; others were engaged, and others like me were starting to venture out into the dating arena. My well-meaning relatives were really looking out for the right match for me. It seemed as if one relative wanted me to marry one man, while others absolutely refused to hear about him. Therefore, I was confused. I asked myself, "Do I have a say in whom I will marry?" In the Burundian culture, it wasn't clear who decided. For our parents' generation, marriages were arranged, so parents and relatives had a big say in the man a girl would marry. More or less, those traditions still apply today, although not as much as they used to. Your family members don't force you to marry someone anymore, but they have a say, or want to have a say. I dated three men before meeting the one I married. Yes, I will tell you more. Here we go.

One afternoon, near the end of my junior year, a man named Claver came to my dorm, carrying a letter for a girl who lived there. Claver was just passing by to deliver the letter, and he didn't know who the girl was. As it turned out, that girl happened to be me! At the time, Claver was an assistant professor of applied sciences at the University of Burundi.

So, after he learned who the letter belonged to, Claver came to my dorm to give it to me. The letter was from Uncle Vincent, who was overseas on a work assignment. He had given that letter to one of his colleagues who happened to be Claver's cousin, and who had just returned from abroad. So Claver came with his sister to bring me my letter; his sister was on the same campus as me and she knew me. After I opened and read the letter, we chatted a little bit. I could see Claver wanted to say something to me, but he looked awkward. After a seemingly agonizing moment, he gathered his courage to ask, "Can we go out and drink tea?"

"Ahh, no thank you; I don't drink tea," I replied.

"Do you prefer coffee?"

"No, I don't drink coffee either."

"Okay, how about water, do you drink water? We can drink water," he persisted.

I looked at him and I wanted to say, "Really, you want to take me out on a date and give me water?" But instead, I said, "No, thank you. I have things to do."

He was disappointed, but he promised he would be back. And he came back the next weekend. I know, I know! I can't believe it myself that he came back, after all the hard time I gave him. Gee, somebody was taking this playing hard to get a little too far. I gave him a hard time until he eventually gave up. Oops!

One year later, we met again unexpectedly, and we started dating. It seemed as if the universe was playing tricks on me because, although my uncle loved me, he had never written to me before. And now, because of his letter, I had found a man!

After Claver and I had dated for about a year, we decided to take the next step and get married. By then, I was in my senior year at the university and we got married in June 1991. After our wedding, my husband and I rented one bedroom in a house we shared with three bachelors; two of them were my husband's best friends. When they learned that I was pregnant, those friends said that my baby would be, without fail, a pretty baby. So they named my unborn baby, *Jolie*, which means "pretty" in French. And they called me "Mama Jolie." The name felt so real and so beautiful; I was proud my womb was carrying such a pretty baby.

It wasn't a small feat to do schoolwork while pregnant, but I passed my finals with flying colors. A month after Jolie was born, my husband received a scholarship to study in Canada for his master's degree in engineering at the university of Sherbrooke, in the province of Quebec, an hour and half south of Montreal. I stayed in Burundi with Baby Jolie to finish my thesis. In Burundi, after you finished your university courses, to receive your bachelor's degree, you also had to present a thesis. A thesis is a long dissertation or essay that usually involves research on a specific topic. My thesis was on Burundi's demographic evolution from the nineteenth century to the 1990s, and I presented it in front of a university jury in February 1992.

• CHAPTER 11 •

Starting from Scratch

AFTER MY THESIS WAS ACCEPTED by the university jury, I was issued a bachelor's degree in literature and human sciences, with a major in history. Quite an accomplishment provided my long way to school. I then started gathering my travel documents to join my husband in Québec, Canada.

Because my husband was a student, I didn't have the right to work at a job. The government of Canada didn't give work permits to spouses of students. That was part of the scholarship agreement. My only job was to take care of the family, and our monthly income was no more than $1,000 US. But because the city of Sherbrooke was small and inexpensive, and our family was still small too, we could manage. The only big institution in the city was the University of Sherbrooke.

My trip to Canada was my first time on an airplane. I was very careful when I walked through the Brussels airport. When I stepped onto the moving walkway, I was sure I would fall and I almost did, with baby Jolie tied on my back, my carry-on luggage in one hand, and my huge winter coat in the other. We spent the night in an airport hotel, but I was too tired to be awed by the hotel's beauty. The next morning, I woke up early to get on the airport shuttle to catch the flight to the Mirabel International Airport in Montreal.

For any newcomer to North America, the first thing that strikes you is the size of things. The roads were way bigger than anywhere else. The size of food in restaurants, the cups, the cars, everything looked big. Even the seasons, especially Québec winters, were colder and longer. At first, I was excited to see the snow. I had only envisioned what snow looked like from my physical geography class at the University of Burundi. In the class, our professor used to tell us many tales about the Western world because he had traveled a lot. Therefore, the image I had of snow was essentially what our professor had taught us in class.

When I arrived in Canada, it was March, so there weren't a lot of snowy days left that year. But I got to see the snow fall twice. However, the accumulated snow on the ground was unbelievable. The city of Sherbrooke was a beautiful green in the summer, but turned into Siberia in the winter. I had never been exposed to so much cold in my life. The cold winter forced me to do what I had never done in Burundi: wear pants. In Burundi, I had never dared to wear them. Country girls, in my time at least, didn't wear pants. It was not considered proper. Pants were normal wear only for city girls, whom I used to envy sometimes. They could wear whatever they liked without being censored. But for a country girl like me, a girl from the village, pants would have been an affront to my family. Sometimes I wore them in my campus dorm room, just to get a feel for what it would be like, but never outside.

It wasn't until I arrived in Canada that I realized pants were the most worn clothing in North America. Now that I was going to have to wear pants because of the weather, it took away all the anticipation I had in wearing them. Pants became my survival outfit, rather than my show-off-your-fashion outfit.

That first year in Québec was quite an adjustment. First, I had to learn about grocery shopping and food prices. When I went to buy groceries, I could not believe how expensive they were, especially since I kept converting each dollar into Burundi francs. Some fruits I had taken for granted my whole life became a luxury. For instance, little blackberries I used to eat fresh off the bushes when I used to herd our cows, now cost a lot, and they weren't even as sweet as what I was used to. Avocados, which were almost free when I lived in Burundi, cost a fortune in Canada and weren't even that good. I had yet to learn to eat the apples that seemed to be the most abundant fruit. I had never seen apples before. Every single food tasted different, and not as good. Definitely, my taste buds had to adjust to my new food, in my new home.

Along with the food adjustment, I had to learn how to cook—I mean on a stove and everything. When I got married, we had a houseboy who cooked, did laundry, and cleaned. Before I got married, I didn't cook because I lived and ate at the university dining hall. And in high school, students didn't have to cook. We did all other chores, except cooking. At home, well, I cooked, but not the same way I would have to cook once in Canada. But step by step, I started to improve my cooking and made edible food.

The language in Québec was another big adjustment. Québec French sounded strange and different from the French I had been taught in school in Burundi. I struggled with comprehension for at least six months. Television programs were my best teachers. After struggling with my listening comprehension, I started to get it. I could finally understand the jokes I watched on the Canadian Broadcasting Corporation (CBC)'s comedy show *"Juste pour Rire* (Just for Laughs)." Once I could understand the jokes, it was a delight to listen to people talk. I never missed that show and was addicted to it every Friday night. At the end of the show was a green cartoon that announced, *"Maman, c'est fini!"* (Mommy, it's over!") I felt disappointed each time the cartoon appeared to end the show. It was the first time I watched someone make fun of politicians (especially the federal prime minister of that time, Jean Chrétien) and get away with it. To me, it was a true testament to democracy.

It was very tough for immigrants to be integrated, even if you spoke French. The five years I lived in Québec were full of fun, though. Universities in Montreal and Québec City had a pool of intellectuals from Burundi who were earning their PhDs in this or that. Very smart people! We quite enjoyed social gatherings, especially on New Year's Eve. On weekends, we took turns inviting other Burundian and Rwandan families who lived in Sherbrooke or friends from Montreal to visit us. So, it didn't feel lonely. We were all full of hopes that, one day, we would return to Burundi with all the credentials we had accumulated and help our country develop. At least that was the aim of most students who received scholarships.

However, the Burundian Civil War of 1993 took away all that hope. Many of the Burundian families living in Canada at that time sought refuge there since they couldn't return home. We had to make a living and started spreading out all over the country to earn it. But the job market was not always friendly when you were an immigrant, and especially a refugee. There were many hurdles, even for highly educated immigrants. You could hold all the degrees in the world, but your skills went unused. Immigrant doctors resorted to driving taxis when they should have been working in the emergency room or operating room, and performing other medical practices. People who used to be in commanding positions in their countries were depressed and had to resign themselves to non-gratifying jobs.

The year 1995 was also a tough time because the province of Québec was trying to secede from Canada and become an independent country. Many immigrants who had become Canadian citizens voted against the separation of Québec from Canada, as did many powerful moneymakers, including big companies, banks, and the financial community in general. As I watched the news every day, I learned that some big Canadian companies were threatening to move their headquarters from Montreal to Toronto, Calgary, Vancouver, or other big financial centers. Some of the US companies established in Québec also projected withdrawing their businesses from an independent Québec. Residents of other provinces were afraid that the separation of one of the biggest Canadian provinces would ignite a disintegration of the whole country, both demographically and economically. Immigrants were particularly anxious, and those who had settled would have to decide whether to leave Québec and start over in other provinces.

In the referendum, the separation proposal—"*Le Non-Québécois*" as it was famously referred to—narrowly lost with a rounded 49 percent of the population voting "Yes" for Québec to withdraw from Canada and 51 percent voting against the motion to secede. Jacques Parizeau, then

Québec's premier, who had initiated the referendum, was very disappointed. In his concession speech, he blamed the "money and the ethnic vote" for the defeat.

Now, if by "ethnic vote," Premier Jacques Parizeau meant that immigrants were partly responsible for preventing Québec from becoming its own country, I think there was some truth in that statement. In many ways, most immigrants came from disintegrated countries, some full of strife and violence, so they didn't want to live in another divided country. From that perspective, Canada couldn't be the beautiful country we knew without Québec in it.

Almost a year after I arrived in Canada, I applied to study business administration. Now as an immigrant, I had the right to work in Canada. But after I tested out the job market, I realized that my degree in history from Burundi wasn't in hot demand. I had gone to the university of Sherbrooke's history department to ask whether I could teach African contemporary history (since it was my major), but I was told by the department's director that it would depend on the students' request for such a class. He encouraged me to prepare the curriculum and wait until the students would request the class. But I didn't want to waste time preparing a curriculum for a class that wasn't being offered on a regular basis.

I decided, instead, I would study what my brother had always wanted me to study —economics. But economics in Burundi didn't seem to hold the same meaning as the economics I was about to study in Canada. In Burundi, the economics faculty combined business and economics classes, but put emphasis on micro- and macro-economics. I decided I really wanted to study something that would open doors for me: business administration. I applied at the University of Sherbrooke, did all the prerequisites, and got admitted into business administration.

Being a mother and a student was difficult, to say the least. But I made a commitment to myself that I would never give up, even if it meant failing some classes and retaking them. I failed big time a class called "Information Systems" in which I was introduced to computers for the first time. Some of the students with whom I took the class were experts even in computer programming. They were fresh out of *Cégep*, which was the equivalent of a two-year junior college. Cégep in French means *Collège d'enseignement général et professionnel*, and in English, it can be translated as *General and Vocational College*. Most Quebec students started their *Cégep* at age seventeen, right after high school. Some chose to just graduate from *Cégep* and entered the workforce with a technical or a vocational degree. But those who chose to receive a bachelor's degree, had to complete two more years at a four-year university.

I also struggled with team assignments. In most classes, we had to form teams for group assignments. When the professor said, "Now it's time to form groups of four or five." All my classmates practically knew each other from their high schools and Cégep, and gathered with their friends to form teams. Shyly, I would ask a team, "Can I join your team?"

"No, we already have enough members." They would say.

I would look left, then right, waiting to see whether anyone was left out like me so we could form a team. But everyone seemed to be part of a team. No one came to me to ask, "Do you want to be on our team?" After, the professor would ask, "Is everyone in teams?" Embarrassed, I would raise my hand and tell the professor I didn't belong to any team.

Usually, the professor would ask, "What team doesn't have four or five members?" The students would grow silent, until the professor picked a team for me to join, as their fifth or sixth member—an overage the team didn't really need. Most of these students had lived in Québec their whole lives and had not even been to Ontario. They weren't used to foreigners, so choosing me, the alien African woman with two kids, just seemed weird to them. Elva, our second child, was born one year after I had started at the University of Sherbrooke.

Although I was still relatively young at twenty-seven, when I started at the University of Sherbrooke, I felt like I was one hundred years old compared to the other students whose average age was nineteen. Being a mother of two and a wife, I had to juggle school and family responsibilities. I was simply not an asset for their teams. Sometimes, I couldn't understand their French, and they probably didn't understand mine either. I envied students who only had to put their efforts into studying and didn't have to split their time and energy with the work at home.

As I advanced to upper grades, I started getting used to the university work, and my grades improved from my usual Cs to B+s, and even occasional As. One of my favorite classes was macro-economics. I loved this class because it taught global economy, monetary systems and other fine theories I strived to learn.

Finally, with hard work and a never, ever give up attitude, I graduated with a bachelor's degree in business administration and a major in finance—just what I wanted!

After we both graduated from the University of Sherbrooke, my husband and I decided to move our family to the city of Toronto, in the province of Ontario. Toronto was a very big city, and I was amazed by how diverse it was. Walking downtown, you could hear five different languages spoken at the same time, any given time.

The first thing I did after we settled in Toronto was to visit the CN Tower. It was quite a discovery for me. First, I felt dizzy because of the height and speed, but once I stepped out of the elevator, what a view! I could see Toronto's entire skyline, the Ontario Place park, Toronto's financial district with its majestic buildings and much more, all from the tower deck. I instantly fell in love with the city. It felt free and outdoorsy. Later, I experienced the subway system— quite a learning experience for a girl who had never ridden trains before. I was lost once in the underground while trying to go shopping at a furniture store. I was sure I knew how to get there; I had written down the stops and street names. One morning after my kids left for school (Baby Jolie was in first grade, no longer a baby obviously, and Elva was in pre-school), I took the bus to the subway. I was feeling confident. When it was time to get off the subway, I couldn't find my exit. I read the map again and again. The train had completed its trip when I realized I had taken the eastbound train instead of the westbound one. I panicked. How was I going to come back and go home? My kids didn't know I was gone, and there was no one home to get them after school.

I asked another passenger, "Why didn't I see my stop?" So, the passenger showed me how to get back on track and get to the westbound train. I didn't make it shopping that day. I was afraid I might get lost again and not make it in time to pick my kids up from school. But there was a certain thrill even in getting lost in the subway system, and you were never alone. I tried again later to navigate Toronto by subway and got around easily after my first attempt. I quite enjoyed browsing and shopping at the Toronto Eaton Centre. Despite its hugeness, Toronto was a livable city.

My husband and I had been looking for jobs in our respective fields of study to no avail. I was working in customer service for an intern's salary, and Toronto was an expensive city. So, we decided to move to a small city in southwestern Ontario, called Windsor, where my husband was able to work in his field. I was then pregnant with Darrel, our third and youngest child. We lived in Windsor for six years, and after twelve years in Canada, our family moved yet again.

In 2004, my family and I relocated to Michigan, a US state at the border of the Canadian city of Windsor. Windsor is so geographically close to the American city of Detroit that you could merge the two into one. Only separated by the Detroit River, it takes about ten minutes to go from one city to the other, either through the tunnel, or over the Ambassador Bridge. Economically, Windsor was an automotive extension of Michigan. Most people in Windsor worked in the automotive industry and depended on it.

When we moved to the United States, I pursued a master's degree in business management (MBA), and thus, started a new journey. After I received my MBA in 2005, I worked in different jobs in finance and accounting in the Detroit area. This was during the economic crisis that began in the 2000s and affected Michigan's automotive industry. I could only find temporary contract jobs in my field of study, and after six years in Michigan, my family and I relocated to Seattle, in the State of Washington.

Education, the Gift that Keeps on Giving

As I shared in this book, education for me was not something accessible; it was something I had to fight for, and never took for granted. Therefore, receiving a master's degree was something I had never thought I could achieve. Education is what exposed me to a much bigger world, all the way from Africa to Canada and then to the United States.

I shared that when I was growing up, I didn't have access to books. So, you can imagine how for a girl who grew up without books, becoming an author was my greatest accomplishment. I can tell you I love books with a vengeance. Writing is my addiction and my passion. I write when I am happy, and I write when I am sad. When I am writing, I even forget to eat. Yeah, imagine that!

In 2013, I published my first book, *Evolving Through Adversity*, which is a longer version of this book for adults. In 2016, I published my second book, a novel titled *A Hand to Hold*. I also published *A Leader's Companion Workbook to Evolving Through Adversity*. This workbook is filled with insights and strategies for overcoming adversity in your personal and professional life.

Along with writing, I travel around the world to share a message of hope, inspire empowerment, and bridge the gaps between our diverse and multicultural communities. I do this several ways through giving conference keynotes, workshops, trainings, seminars, and speaking at various events.

One topic I'm passionate about is *Diversity and Inclusion*. I know too well how being excluded can feel. Being an African immigrant woman, I have had my share of disillusions, exclusions, and being discriminated against. I have had my share of racism, sexism, and all the other isms. But in those challenges, I also found my passion for educating people about each other's differences and how to bridge communities with a common purpose. I facilitate diversity events in schools, colleges, and organizations to spark a conversation about social issues. I also give presentations on leadership and resilience to inspire and empower people on how to overcome the adversities in life, using a unique transformational model I call, *RRU Model*™. *RRU* stands for: Reflect – Rectify – Unite.

The truth is I couldn't do the work I do without education. School has allowed me to learn and grow. Now, I am paying it forward to use my education and help make the world a better place for all, one book, one reader, and one audience at a time. And I owe it to those who paved the way for me to go to school, those who paid for my school fees, and those who were my teachers, both in the formal and informal sense.

As a speaker, I share stories that unite us all and make us relatable to one another, no matter a person's race, gender, sexual orientation, religion, national origin, political affiliation, age, or any other identity background. At our very core, we all yearn to be accepted for who we are, and to be able to use our God-given talents and live up to our full potential.

In 2016, I gave a TEDx talk titled, "We Are Not All That Different." I truly believe we are far more alike than different. You can watch it on YouTube; just type in my full name and it will come up.

I am also an advocate for girls' education, speaking up against practices like child marriage, domestic violence against women and other cultural hindrances that rob many girls and women of the opportunity to learn and be all they can be. That's why I love speaking in schools to remind young people about the importance of getting a good education. The privilege of being able to attend school is not something many kids around the world have. I want to open a conversation with students in the Western world on how others around the world live, and the power Western students have to make a positive impact in other youths' lives.

That is why I shared my story in this book, and I couldn't have written this book without an education. Education gave me a chance to use my gifts and better learn how to achieve my fullest potential. My hope is that young readers of all backgrounds can reflect on who they are and where they fit into the scheme of life. They will learn how to identify and use their gifts, and how to be the change makers they wish to see in the world. New generations have tremendous power because of technology's advancement, but many youths live in isolation, unaware of what happens in other parts of the world. Humanity is intertwined, and every human deserves a chance to achieve his or her potential. We all want the same across races and cultures: to be accepted for who we are, and to use our gifts to uplift ourselves, our families, and our whole world.

I believe education is the only solution that truly empowers communities and has the potential to end the cycle of poverty. Because of my education, I was able to earn a living and money to build a nice home for my parents and support them financially before they passed away. Our family home now has electricity, thanks to solar power technology. That is something I never thought my family would have. The truth is none of this would have happened if it were not for the education my brothers and I received. In my life, education has been the gift that keeps on giving.

You might be asking, "Is education in Burundi better today?" While today in Burundi they don't pay school fees in primary school as they did in my time, the infrastructures have not been improved, and as the population has increased, more people are sending their kids to school. Today, Burundi ranks as one of the least developed countries in the world, which makes it hard for schools to innovate. As in many African countries, education in Burundi is still inaccessible for many families. Because of the lack of school materials and space, such as classrooms and desks, students cannot all be accommodated, and only those whose parents can afford private education are likely to carry on and go to high school. Even those who advance to high school still have to pay tuition, and not many families can afford it. But Burundian kids are as smart as anyone; they just don't have the opportunities to go to school or stay in school, or even use their skills once they finish school.

And when it comes to educating girls, that challenge is even bigger. By customary laws, everything a family owns exclusively belongs to the father. That's how the system was, and still is in many cases. Many women don't have any ownership rights in terms of land rights or any other rights for that matter. To know about those rights, you have to be educated, and many women and girls are illiterate. For many parents, the only vision they have for their daughters is to marry them off, which only continues to perpetrate the cycle of poverty and abuse of women.

I knew I was challenging the system when I demanded education. I was challenging a culture that considers girls and women as second-class citizens. This belief causes many social issues that go hand-in-hand with women's lack of education and rights, such as violence against women and child marriage.

Today, we know that providing girls with a good education is vital for a country's development. When women are educated and can share in making decisions about their families and how to earn their living, the whole country benefits because the standard of living improves, as does society's overall health. It is often said that when you educate a girl, not only do you change her life and her family's, but you also change her community, her country, and her world. Therefore, it is important to let girls learn.

I hope this book gives you the inspiration and motivation to follow through in school, even when it's super-hard. I hope you never, *ever* give up. There were many times when I was tempted to just call it quits because it was hard. For example, walking to high school for two days across the deep valleys and on the big mountain was super hard for me, but I never gave up. If I had, you wouldn't be reading this book.

As you continue to grow and walk on your journey, you will discover that even when things are going well, it doesn't mean you will not face some challenges. Life is a constant balancing act of good and bad, right and wrong, ups and downs, and everything in between. Changing times will always require evolving mindsets. You can rest assured that you are stronger than you think, and you can overcome any adversity. Keep your head up and your integrity intact. You came into this world with unique talents, and the world can't wait to see the expression of those talents. Follow your passion and fulfill your purpose.

I believe everybody needs a little encouragement in life, no matter how old you are. That is why I love to write and speak—so I can share stories to encourage you to do and be the best you can. Never forget that you are here on Earth for a reason. Don't let anyone or anything stand in your way of achieving your dreams. Always be persistent, like I was, even though it was *a long way to school*.

Ten Leadership Habits for the Teen Years and Beyond

Before you work on the following reflection questions, let me first share ten good habits you can develop as you navigate life in your teen years and beyond.

1. **Mind Your Words:** Words have a significant impact in our lives. They have the power to bless or hurt, whether it's blessing or hurting us or others. Through your words, you can change your life or someone else's. Some stereotypes and biases come from using words that can denigrate a person or a group of people because of their race, culture, nationality, religion, or disabilities. So, be mindful of the words you use when speaking of yourself or others.

2. **Think Before You Act:** Responding is different from re-acting (re-acting). It is better to respond than to react. When someone or something irritates you, before you

respond, take a deep breath while counting to four backwards, and then respond appropriately. Having self-control in the way you respond to situations will help you be in control of yourself.

3. **Be Clear in Your Intentions:** Say what you mean and mean what you say. Some people think that in order not to hurt someone's feelings, you have to lie to that person. They say a bunch of words that mean nothing, just to escape telling the truth. Be upfront, but tell the truth in a kind way. The person's feelings might be hurt, but in the long run, they will be better off than believing in the lies.

4. **Address Issues in the Moment:** What you don't deal with never heals. Especially in relationships, we've all been in situations when we didn't deal with something hurtful in the moment it happened, and then we carry that pain for a very long time. Then later, we realize that the other person has probably forgotten what they did. And when you bring it back, they are like, "What are you talking about?" Try to deal with issues as they arise, instead of suppressing them, and then move on.

5. **Garbage In Is Garbage Out:** Watch what you feed your mind. In computer programming, there is a saying, "*Garbage in, garbage out.*" In simple words, what that means is what you put into your computer program-

ming is what you will get out of it. If you put garbage in, you get garbage out. And if it is good stuff, then you will get good stuff out as well. So be careful what you put in your mind. Always make sure you try to feed your mind on good stuff, so you can get good stuff out of it. Feed on good mind-food.

6. **Renew the Garbage Bag:** Imagine if at home we never emptied the garbage bag and put in a new one. What odors would we have to smell? Awful, right? It is the same with our minds. Even being the best of the best, you will still have to deal with life circumstances that can leave your mind full of junk and negativity. So, how can you renew your mind, and empty the stinky bag? I recommend using a journal to write down your negative emotions and feelings. After you've emptied the stinky emotions, you will need to fill your mind with good stuff. So, take some time to reflect and write down the good things you have in your life, and what you are grateful for. As I already shared in the prologue, find good inspirational messages that can replace the negative messages that tend to harass your mind.

7. **Acknowledge What You Can or Cannot Control:** From what you've written in your diary, see if there are things you can change to make the situation better, and then change those things. But also, acknowledge

what you cannot control or change, and let it be. If you can't change it, let it go!

8. **Be You, the Best You:** Don't spend time wishing you were someone else or working to change someone else's behaviors. You are only responsible for your own behaviors. If you are doing good at treating yourself and others with kindness and respect, what you do can inspire others to change for the better, but it has to be their responsibility, not yours. Everybody has stuff to deal with, so work on yourself.

9. **Love Who You Are and Be Your Own Best Friend First:** When the world seems to be self-absorbed with their own issues, don't just follow the trend so you can have likes on social media by posting stuff that might hurt you or others. Instead, be your own advocate, your own best friend. Seek help when you need it. Reach out to get another perspective from those you trust, to help you cope with pain in healthy ways. Become a voice that prevents bullying, peer pressure, experimenting with drugs, abusing alcohol, and other self-destructing behaviors, whether in school or out of school.

10. **Choose Your Relationships Wisely:** When you are young, especially in your teen years, relationships have a huge importance in your life. Look at your current relationships. Whether they are romantic relationships

or simple friendships, are they nurturing you to grow and be the best you can be? Look at what the relationship is doing in your life. A relationship that is demeaning, degrading, or toxic is not good for you. A relationship that demands you do things you know are bad in any way, and causes you to do those things so you can have someone in your life, is definitely not good for you. No one should make you do anything without your full consent. People tend to become like the people they hang out with. In the end, you are responsible for the choices you make. Remember *free will*?

Overall, try to make good choices, because no matter what your mom and dad say or do, no matter what your teachers and educators tell you, at the end of the day, once you step out of that door, at home or at school, the choice is all yours. And so are the rewards or the consequences of your actions. Having free will also means you have personal power, so use that power for good. You are a leader, so lead yourself in the right direction.

As you venture out into the world, open your mind to learning about new things such as different cultures and how other people think and act. Check your own biases and stereotypes; we all have them. But don't let them dictate who you become. Evolve instead and shift your mindset whenever necessary. Reach out and build relationships with those you perceive as different; teach them what you know that they don't, and learn from them what they know that you don't.

In the next section, I have added some reflection questions for you to work on and explore your story. Take a journal or a diary and answer the following questions. There is no wrong answer. This is only to help you reflect on your story and discover who you really are. If you need help, ask your parents/guardians to help you with some of the things you may not know yet.

Enjoy the process!

Reflection Questions

1. **Childhood Memories**

a. What childhood memories do you have that are shaping how you are growing up?

_____

_____

_____

b. Who are the people involved in those memories and how influential are they in your life?

_____

_____

_____

c. What have you learned from those memories that can help you become a stronger you?

_____

_____

_____

2. **Family Roots**

a. Take a moment to reflect on your roots; do you know your origins?

_____

_____

_____

b. Ask your parents or guardians whether there was a time when they had mixed or conflicting feelings about their origins.

_____

_____

_____

c. If so, what did those feelings and emotions ignite in them?

_____

_____

_____

3. **Acknowledging History**

a. Were you or your parents ever affected by any war, any time in your lives?

_____

_____

_____

b. If so, which one, and how did you/your parents cope?

_____

_____

_____

c. Looking back on your own country's history, do you
    see anything that may have impacted you as part of
    your personal history? For instance, did you or do you
    attend a school where you feel discriminated against,
    or where you are made to feel different? Or maybe you
    have witnessed others being discriminated against
    while you were among the privileged group? Take a
    moment and reflect on that. How does this affect how
    you view yourself and others, and what can you do to
    make the world a better place for all?

    _____

    _____

    _____

    _____

    _____

4. Losing Loved Ones

a. Losing my grandmother was the first time I experi-
    enced the death of someone I deeply loved. Is there a
    situation that has affected you in a painful way? What
    was it?

    _____

    _____

    _____

b. What did you learn from that situation?

    _____

    _____

    _____

c.   How might you use what you learned from that situation to help yourself and others?

_____

_____

_____

5.   Family Dynamics

a.   You have probably heard the quote, (attributed to Harper Lee, from the novel, *To Kill a Mockingbird*), "You can choose your friends, but you cannot choose your family." Family dynamics have a tremendous impact on our lives. Describe your relationship with your parents.

_____

_____

_____

_____

_____

b.   How is your relationship with your siblings?

_____

_____

_____

_____

c.   What did/does your family teach you that continues to shape who you are?

_____

_____

_____

6. Education

a. What do you want to be when you grow up?

_____

_____

_____

b. Is college something you want to pursue? If so, what do you plan to study?

_____

_____

_____

c. What are your natural talents, and how can you use them to pursue your dreams?

_____

_____

_____

Acknowledgments

One of the greatest joys of my life is that I get to do work I'm passionate about. Since I first published *Evolving Through Adversity*, I have had many good inspirational moments to write and create content, and I have also had many speaking engagements to share that content and inspire and empower others on their life journeys.

As I continue to meet diverse audiences, both young and old, one of the topics I enjoy sharing is Diversity and Inclusion. I try to approach this topic with an open mind, and I have had the joy of meeting all kinds of people of different racial, sexual, cultural, and religious backgrounds. I have had the pleasure of sharing different insights and perspectives, as well as learning from my audience members. The truth is that we can all learn from and empower one another on our life journeys, and be the light the world around us needs. So, it is with deep gratitude that I express my heartfelt appreciation to:

- My parents, who gave me not just life, but one that's full of writing material, and who are now watching over me from their afterlife.

- My brothers and sisters, who just by being my siblings, enrich every work I create.

- My husband and my children, for their acceptance, love, and support as I pursue my passion for sharing stories that inspire others.

- The many organizational leaders, for allowing me to share diverse stories from diverse perspectives.

- My editor, Tyler Tichelaar, for his sharp eye for detail.

About the Author

Seconde Nimenya is the award-winning author of *Evolving Through Adversity: How to Overcome Obstacles, Discover Your Passion, and Honor Your True Self*, a story of her life journey and the life lessons she has learned along the way.

Her second book, *A Hand to Hold*, is a novel of love, healing, and redemption. And her third book, *A Leader's Companion Workbook to Evolving Through Adversity*, is filled with leadership insights and strategies for personal and professional development.

Seconde is an inspirational speaker and a diversity and inclusion trainer and advocate. With twenty years of multicultural leadership experience, Seconde is a leader on diversity and inclusion in the workplace and educational institutions, debunking stereotypes and biases, and sharing skills on resilience and overcoming adversities to grow personally and professionally.

Burundi-born and raised, Seconde came to the United States by way of Canada. She uses her multinational and multicultural background to inspire and empower her audiences, and she is considered one of the noted motivational speakers in her field.

Seconde is a TEDx speaker on race and culture, and her TEDx talk "We Are Not All that Different" continues to inspire people worldwide. In the talk, Seconde makes the case that despite being different, people have more in common than what separates them.

In 2017, Seconde was honored with the "**Seeds of Hope Award**" by RESULTS for her work in sharing a message of tolerance and bridging the gaps between our diverse and multicultural communities.

In 2019, Seconde also received the "**Bold and Resilient Woman Award,"** honoring her for her work and contributions in inspiring leadership resilience and bridging the gaps between diverse and multicultural communities. She has been featured in various media outlets such as TV, radio, magazines, newspapers, and other publications in the United States and around the world.

For more information about Seconde Nimenya and her work, or to purchase copies of her books, visit:
www.SecondeNimenya.com

Invite Seconde Nimenya To Speak at Your Next Event

Using thought-provoking and powerful principles, Seconde Nimenya's presentations will impact how your teams interact at work and in life, getting them to think in new and creative ways. Her topics work well as keynotes, workshops, or seminars.

Seconde's presentations entertain as they educate, leaving your audience wanting more out of life and work.

To book Seconde to speak, send an email to:
info@SecondeNimenya.com

For more information, visit:
www.SecondeNimenya.com

Praise for
Evolving Through Adversity

"This book is great and so inspiring. I can't even imagine moving halfway across the world and readjusting to a new culture. I really enjoyed reading Evolving Through Adversity."

— **Tyler R. Tichelaar, Ph.D., award -winning author of**
When Teddy Came to Town

"If you are looking for a resource to give you hope and for overcoming all life's adversities, then, start here!"

— **Patrick Snow, international best-selling author of**
Creating Your Own Destiny

"What a gift! Written by an extraordinary woman who, through much adversity, finds incredible potential within herself. This book is filled with lessons of perseverance and hope, beneficial to everyone."

— **Susan Friedmann, CSP, international best-selling**
author of *Riches in Niches*

"*Evolving Through Adversity* is an example of how we can't love and honor others, without first loving and honoring ourselves. Love comes from within, and this book teaches us how to find it."

— **B. Imei Hsu, LMHC, Founding Counselor of**
Seattle Direct Counseling

"Growing up in a culture completely unlike our own, we learn about the experiences of a little girl whose pain and history shaped her into who she is today."

— **Joe Raymond**

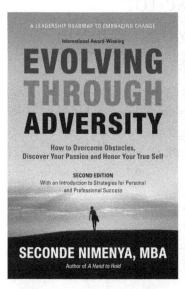

A LEADERSHIP ROADMAP TO EMBRACING CHANGE

International Award-Winning

EVOLVING THROUGH ADVERSITY

How to Overcome Obstacles,
Discover Your Passion and Honor Your True Self

SECOND EDITION
With an Introduction to Strategies for Personal
and Professional Success

SECONDE NIMENYA, MBA
Author of *A Hand to Hold*

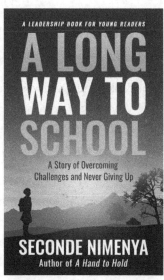

A LEADERSHIP BOOK FOR YOUNG READERS

A LONG WAY TO SCHOOL

A Story of Overcoming
Challenges and Never Giving Up

SECONDE NIMENYA
Author of *A Hand to Hold*

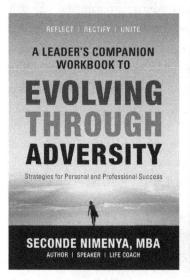

REFLECT | RECTIFY | UNITE

A LEADER'S COMPANION WORKBOOK TO

EVOLVING THROUGH ADVERSITY

Strategies for Personal and Professional Success

SECONDE NIMENYA, MBA
AUTHOR | SPEAKER | LIFE COACH

A HAND TO HOLD

SECONDE NIMENYA
International award-winning author of *EVOLVING THROUGH ADVERSITY*

9 781733 112406